From Dinner Date to Soulmate

Cynthia Spillman's Guide to Mature Dating

Cynthia Spillman

Published by Bennion Kearny Limited
6 Woodside
Churnet View Road
Oakamoor
ST10 3AE

www.BennionKearny.com

Cover images of Cynthia Spillman by Christopher Ratcliffe

For Peter, with all my love, for teaching me to embrace and
live life with outrageous passion, for being my greatest supporter, and for
enabling me to connect to a joie de vivre and level of happiness, I never dared
believe was possible. Long may we continue to ride side by side, backwards,
blindfolded, on the exciting rollercoaster, which is our relationship.

ABOUT CYNTHIA SPILLMAN

Cynthia Spillman is Chief Executive of The International Dating Academy, a one stop dating shop for people who wish to improve their dating skills. She was formerly Chief Executive of Dinner Dates, the UK's top social networking club for elite professional singletons. Her area of expertise is in mindful dating. Her articles have been published in a number of magazines including Vogue, Woman's Own and online magazine Single Living. She is also an award winning inspirational trainer and motivational speaker. She has kissed a lot of frogs in her time, but is now happily married to her third husband, Peter. She divides her time between London and Nice.

www.cynthiaspillman.co.uk

www.internationaldatingacademy.com

ACKNOWLEDGEMENTS

My deepest gratitude goes to the following, special people, who have never stopped rooting for me:

Sam Targett, my extraordinary daughter, for putting up with me for 37 years, for demonstrating to me daily, what true courage really is, and for turning out so amazingly well, despite having me as her mother.

Connie Targett, my beautiful granddaughter, and the most spectacular proof that miracles truly do happen.

My wider family in the UK, US and Nice – my sister Martine Stone, cousins Vicki and Ed Crawford, Jean-Luc and Ajda Barnoin, Janie Barnoin and Catherine Sennhauser, for always believing in me and for showing me love and light, during the darkest days of my life – and on many occasions since then.

My faithful "Parkies" – my Glasgow childhood school friends Anne Ng Ping Cheung, Gail Squires and Noelle Low. Also, Elaine Wilson, my valiant convent school co-survivor. I feel so lucky to have you all in my life.

My much-loved "old" friends, Shirley Hagart and Kathy and Ken Hamilton, who remind me that I once did have a son called Anthony, and who enable me to still honour his memory, 30 years later, by often talking about him with me.

Sherry and John Cross, for being with, and helping me on that catastrophic day in November 1987, and for still being such a nurturing part of our lives, all these years later.

My smart and beautiful Cambridge University girlfriends and former fellow law students, Carole Watts and Clare Glendinning for supporting me so much and indulging me in my wild phase, so soon after my life had fallen apart. Long may we continue to lunch and laugh together.

Judy Lax, for the deep, unbreakable bond we share as bereaved mothers, and for the many years of Sisterhood Therapy, over numerous cups of coffee, lunches and via SOS texts.

My "special and different" friends Debbie and Chris, who, somehow, keep me on the straight and narrow, with great humour. And for the other members of my tribe – you know who you are.

Frieda de Ley, my patient and skilled business coach, and early "midwife", who helped me give birth to the notion of this book – "I was lost, now I'm found!"

Dragana Djukic, my inspirational mindfulness trainer, and most importantly, my compassionate witness.

Ghazala-Aziz Scott, physician extraordinaire, and now one of my most nurturing, loving friends.

And last, but definitely not least – my fantastic publisher, James Lumsden-Cook, who was willing to "take a walk on the wild side" with this book. You won't regret it!

TABLE OF CONTENTS

PART 3: MOVING FROM FIRST DATE TO SOULMATE

INTRODUCTION

Who I am, and why I wrote this book on mature dating

Are you sick to the back teeth of searching for Mr Right, and forever ending up with Mr Wrong? Do you feel despondent, weary, and about to throw in the towel? If so, this is definitely the book for you.

My motivation for writing this guide to love at any age was fuelled by a profound desire to empower women to dig themselves out of mental apathy and deliver results-orientated action. This is a road map for women who find themselves, for whatever reason, searching for a partner in mid or later life.

I know it's not always easy. I married my third husband, Peter, when I was 48.

For many years, I was the Chief Executive of Dinner Dates, the UK's longest-established networking organisation for high-end professional single people, and I had countless experiences of helping women to find love. In turn, after Dinner Dates, I set up The International Dating Academy, a one-stop-shop, for people who want to improve their dating skills. These two businesses have put me in a unique to position to help older women find long-term contentment with the right partner.

Why this book is essential

Like many women, I have (in the past) found myself to be *"relationship-challenged"*. In other words, we keep banging our heads against a brick wall in our love search, to the point where we really start to believe that we're going to end up lonely old ladies with cats for company.

We're human and we make mistakes, and as we age it can feel petrifying even to contemplate re-entering the relationship jungle.

When you're in the jungle, you need a guide.

After a considerable amount of research, I realised that there's a dearth of mature dating self-help books for women. I decided that the time had come for me to produce my own route map for women; after all, I'm only too familiar with how

1

jaded and disillusioned we can become when we're searching for love. I come at this book from an empathetic and compassionate heart set. I've walked the walk and, in mid-bloom, am blossoming more than ever before.

Asking for help is a sign of strength, a real badge of courage. You outsource your tax affairs to your accountant, or you work with a personal trainer – well I'm a personal trainer for people looking for love. There's an effective and a *mindful* way of going about the search for a partner or a slap-dash, hit and miss approach. I hope you opt for the former! Your time is valuable, and your happiness is precious – so please make space in your busy schedule and join me on this awesome journey.

It's my mission to help you overcome your fears, frustration and apathy, by providing you with a clear blueprint for the journey to finding and keeping love – at any age.

Who this mature dating book is for

This book is dedicated to single women, separated women and widowed and bereaved women of all shapes, sizes and life situations. Perhaps you're already enjoying a great life, and the cherry on the cake would be finding a fabulous man to share it with. Maybe you've been so badly hurt by a previous partner that you've shied off ever being intimate again – yet in your soul, you instinctively know that love heals all pain. Dare to try again.

Or perhaps you've been way too consumed by building your career to have found the time to seek love actively. You may even feel that love has passed you by and that it's too late. Nonsense! It's never too late. There's always hope, and in the following pages you'll find answers, as well as facts and figures, which will shake your misconceptions to the core. Prepare to be challenged, as I deconstruct the many myths which lurk in the way of the mature woman finding relationship joy.

How this book will help you

Fundamentally, happiness is an *Inside Job*. I'm going to lead you through a comprehensive three-step journey which will dramatically increase your chances of reaching your intended destination: love and emotional enrichment.

Part one, step one, "Be prepared", is all about preparing yourself for love because, if you're not happy in yourself, you certainly won't find contentment through a man, nor will you attract the right partner for you. By doing the *Inner Work, more than anything else you do*, you will not only feel happier in any event, but you will bring about a quantum improvement in attracting the kind of man *who's actually right for you*. Without doing the groundwork you could register with every online site in the world, you might well meet men, you will probably have dates… but will you find a soulmate and live happily ever after? I don't think so!

Part two, "How to find potential partners", shows you where and how to find the man of your dreams. It provides you with a multifaceted approach to finding *The One*.

Part three, "Moving from first date to soulmate", spells out the vital ingredients for lasting relationship success.

My mature dating methods are tried and tested. This isn't a book which is to be read and then stuck back on the shelf without further action. When I work on a one-to-one basis with clients, I use a systematic approach; as you and I are not face to face, I'll adapt the way I work so that you too can benefit.

Loving again after loss, and practising relationship mindfulness

This book is also unique in two further ways, both of which are extremely relevant to mid-lifers. I dedicate an entire chapter to loving again after loss, be it following on from separation, divorce or widowhood. Having the ability and tools to do this, and to make space for new love, is crucial. I also include a section on practising relationship mindfulness. Mindfulness is the new buzz word of our decade. Far from being the latest wishy-washy New Age fad, it's a scientifically-proven mechanism for fostering inner growth. Mindfulness is powerful, yet simple – a transformative tool in our emotional and spiritual bag of tricks. Note that when I employ the term *"spiritual"*, this is absolutely nothing to do with religion, rather a change in the way we learn to perceive the world, and each other. To the best of my knowledge, there's no other dating skills book of this kind, encompassing both aspects.

Labels are for jars and not people. *You're not past it*, no matter what figure your birth certificate may state. I promise you that if you accompany me on this journey to love, and you follow my suggestions and take continuous action – you too will be rewarded with the enormous joy that I (and many people that I have coached) have found. It's our birthright to live, and love, outrageously. Grab your courage with both hands, and enjoy the mature dating ride!

PART 1

BE PREPARED

CHAPTER 1

THE FIRST PERSON YOU NEED TO
GET TO KNOW. YOURSELF!

Let's start off with a tough question: Would you be happier staying single?

How do you feel about this question? You may have done an immediate double-take, horrified by its sheer temerity. You may even have experienced a deep surge of indignation – it's blindingly obvious that you're not happy being single. Otherwise, you wouldn't have bought this book!

Indulge me in playing devil's advocate for a moment.

Ninety percent of our emotions are concealed in the subconscious. Things are rarely as simple as they initially seem, and although it's going to evoke controversy, I believe that some people just aren't cut out for coupledom. If you work your way through this book, using my suggested tools, and you do come to that conclusion, then I salute you and wish you a splendid life where the things you need come from people and other stimuli in your life; other than that one "special" person! Love is blind, but relationships are an eye-opener.

If, however, you're up for some radical self-challenging and self-transformational action, and you discover that you *really* do want to find a partner, then this is absolutely the book for you.

The Inside Job Principle

Most "How to Find Love" books adopt, what I believe, to be a superficial and facile approach to your love search, focusing purely on externals such as having a certain type of man, worrying what others think of us, and competing with other women on the man hunt. Actually, we have little control over these things. That's because the only person we can ever truly control – and change – is ourselves. My approach is based on what has *actually worked* for me personally, for my clients, and for many friends and relatives. I come at it from a completely different and unique, sassy, heart-set.

The most important, yet neglected, element on the path to finding a permanent enriching relationship, is *You*. If you don't love and care first and foremost for yourself, you'll have no chance of loving somebody else. Smart singletons are far likelier to find and keep love if they've undertaken *The Work* on themselves, before they venture out into the big, wide relationship world on their love quest.

Self-fulfilled single ladies are more attractive to potential partners, and more likely to go on to form happy couples. The reverse is also true. If you skip the stage of getting yourself sorted, the relationship will be built on weak foundations, whereas if you're *really* sorted (and so is your choice of partner), your relationship will be built on rock.

Alexander Graham Bell said, "Before anything else, *preparation* is the key to success." How much time, emotional energy and money would you put into planning your wedding day – a single day? Ergo – how much should you put into finding that person you'd want to spend the rest of your life with? The answer is surely a no-brainer! So, my very loud message is that for now, you *must* keep the spotlight entirely on *you*, and not focus on looking for a man.

Nobody can ever make you feel complete and whole, other than yourself. Whilst you may believe and experience rough external circumstances, and automatically conclude that these must dictate your reactions, as the great Viktor Frankl, concentration camp survivor, and pioneer of Logotherapy stated, "The last aspect of humanity which can be stripped from a person is that of *choice*."

I'm going to show you how to make wiser partner choices. When I refer to The Inside Job or FLY Principle, I mean that unless you love yourself first, then you'll never be able to love anybody else. You have to do the inner work, so that first and foremost you feel content in yourself.

The art and practice of nurturing self-care

Practising the art of nurturing self-care ebbs effortlessly, like a river tributary, into the *Inside Job* principle, and must consequently be stage one in finding love. Sure, a great partner can transform your world. But ultimately, only you can choose your feelings. How many celebrities do we know who objectively seem to have it all, but are actually prey to depression, compulsion and misery?

Confidence, which goes hand in hand with practising self-care, is also an *Inside Job*. If you feel good about yourself, this will spill over everywhere, making you a more alluring potential companion in the process. You can't 'give' from a place of emotional emptiness.

Think of the oxygen mask principle. When you get on a plane, and the flight attendant runs through the safety instructions, you're advised to put on YOUR mask first, before you try to help anybody else. This analogy applies in the arena of love. Think FLY – First Love Yourself – and others will then follow.

Remember – nobody can ever complete you. The relentless search for that missing "whole," in order to make you complete, falls under the label of co-dependency, a subject about which I could write a veritable tome.

If you throw your lot in *totally* with your *Significant Other*, you suck them and the relationship dry, because effectively you're not growing as an individual in your own right. Foolishly, you are attempting to get all your succour and validation from a man, so you end up being swallowed up by a bigger whole and lose your own powerful self in the process. This is why it's absolutely crucial that you do learn to practise the art of nurturing self-care, and I'll identify ways for you to do just that throughout the book.

And doing that involves not just "the externals" but – much more importantly – defining, and acting upon, "the internals" which include: motivation, perception, and attitudes.

You can't afford to skip this essential first step of identifying the internals. It will begin the process of constructing emotional resilience, which you're going to need in shovelfuls when you do start dating again.

If you find yourself already baulking at these preliminary suggestions, then allow me to point out that perhaps your motivation levels aren't what they could be. Without renewed, daily, rigorous self-motivation, the chances of reaching love Nirvana are nil; as brutal as this may sound. There will be much more on motivation in subsequent chapters. For the moment, keep calm and carry on reading.

I now invite you to consider which of these statements apply to your current personal situation, to verify you truly don't want to remain single. You may think that some of them are slightly tongue-in-cheek, but truth is often expressed in jest. This exercise will help you to decide what you *really* want as opposed to what you *think* you want.

Own your true feelings by candidly completing the sentences which follow this paragraph, with whichever statements apply to you. Write them down! It's no wonder the saying goes, "The pen is mightier than the sword." Journaling is a self-empowering, vital and integral part of this journey. Writing things down the good old-fashioned way, with pen on paper, is a fabulous way of processing and clarifying your thoughts and feelings.

Over a period of time, you start to observe patterns of behaviour and attitudes and, hopefully, you learn from them. Journaling is also important in that you can keep yourself motivated by looking back and realising just how far you've come. We'll be setting SMART dating goals (Specific, Measurable, Achievable, Realistic, Time-specific), along the way.

Don't sabotage your chances at the off. Writing is thinking on paper. There's something almost magical about having a special journal in which you write everything down by hand. It's as if there's a connection between the heart and the pen, which can't be replicated with modern-day technology. Now, without further ado:

"A long-term partner would provide me with…"

Companionship on the journey through life

Well, it's true that the right partner will be great company, but you have to make a wise choice. The French say, "It's better to travel alone, than to be badly accompanied." Get wise, get focused and get real about your prospects. If this statement applies to you, write it down in your journal!

Status and competitive positioning – keeping up with Mrs Jones

Come on! All that glitters isn't gold. Status can vary over a lifetime and really isn't a big deal. Competition is rarely a helpful tactic because it can puncture an already flagging or fragile level of self-esteem. In turn, when, where, and how do you decide to stop competing and comparing? Competing in this area of your life really doesn't serve you. Everyone's journey is different.

Celia was a 50-year-old lecturer. Despite my setting her tasks, in an attempt to move her forward in her love life, she put up fierce objection after objection. When challenged, I was treated to a load of "buts" and "becauses" – in other words, flimsy excuses for justifying staying stuck. When a client presents me with the latter, it translates to, "I've heard everything you've just said, *but* I can't be arsed to take any of it on board. After several frustrating sessions, we were able to extrapolate from the "noise" that actually she didn't want a man right now, because she was fully-occupied undertaking research for a PhD. She thought she wanted a man, because she was comparing herself to everyone else, and finding herself lacking. I pointed out to her that this wasn't actually a failure – merely the realisation that, at the moment, she has other priorities in her life – and that's perfectly okay!

Sex – a permanent hot date 24/7, 365 days a year

Most people understandably rate the pleasures of the flesh highly. But you don't need a permanent partner to enjoy good, safe and uncomplicated sex. Steamy sex on its own won't sustain a relationship for the long haul. It eventually burns out, and all that you're left with is a carcass of "a relationship." Enduring, fantastic sex, however, is eminently possible within a nurturing long term relationship. It oils the wheels – but again doesn't happen without ongoing imagination and work.

Someone to grow old with

To share a bed with your beloved until the meat wagon eventually comes to fetch one of you is a noble ambition. But being entwined with *Mr Wrong* can be a lifelong prison sentence, with no obvious parole card.

Emotional and financial security

And why not? Emotional and financial security can be the springboard for many joint and individual lifetime adventures, BUT you have to communicate honestly, openly and tactfully about the agreed parameters for both emotional and financial issues. Any "slippage" in understanding could result in a Day of Reckoning, resulting in relational trauma.

Nobody, ultimately, benefits if their partner engages in financial misadventure or any variation on adultery. It's important to establish flexible boundaries and agree them as and when needed. You also need to reflect upon how you'll feel giving up total independence and control of your life – both physically and money-wise. How would it grab you, being accountable to your partner? He'd be in your face for good, so how would it feel to lose your space in every sense of the word? There's no such thing as a free lunch.

A sense of completeness

I reckon this chestnut must spring from 1950's movies and songs. I repeat – nobody can ever make you feel complete. A relationship can afford you opportunities which eluded you as a single person, but if you forget that you were once – and still are – a separate person from your partner (with a separate, unique identity), then your relationship may hit the rocks downstream; nobody likes to be held hostage to another. Nor is a melodramatic fear of being alone to be cited as a reason for needing a man. In this day and age, you can be alone, but need never be lonely.

The cherry on top of my existing cake and successful life

I adore nice, bright red cherries – but when they sit on the top of a cake, they get gobbled up first – and then you have to ask yourself: do you really like what's left of the cake? The point being that relationships are fabulous, but they're also a bit like buying a brand new car. At first, there's huge excitement, and you make an enormous effort to keep the car clean. But before you know it, that shiny and new feeling wears off, and you're left with a car that starts developing lots of flaws and imperfections. The same analogy applies to a relationship. You're on a hormonal high, but then you get used to each other, and the mundane takes over. Morning breath and bathroom smells are all part of the daily humdrum of relationship life. Are you being realistic about your expectations? It's not all romance and roses around the door 24/7.

Someone with whom to share my joys and sorrows

If you've lived this long, then you already have someone to do just that. She's called a girlfriend. In fact, you probably have more than one, and there's no finer support network than The Sisterhood. A good man is a wonderful adjunct to this but, all too often, women find a life partner and wave "adieu" to their female support network. This is extremely foolhardy. Don't do it. Whether you're in or out of a relationship, always make spending time and communicating with your girlfriends a top priority.

Expansion of my social circle and interests

Rest assured, you're going to be doing plenty of this during your love search, if indeed you do decide that you still want a man! You should never stop expanding your social circle, even when you're in a committed relationship. You'll keep re-energising yourself, your partner, and your union, if you do.

Healing the emotional damage of my past

I know it to be true... love is a many splendored thing. The right love can open lots of doors and it can help heal emotional scars. But the mistake that many make is to transform a partner into a therapist. You can't and shouldn't expect your partner to heal your deep-rooted trauma. That's the specialist work of a therapist or 12-step programme. There's plenty of support out there, so if you're stuck in a deep hole, please stop digging and seek it. There's a list of resources at the end of this book.

Men aren't for dumping on. What guy, when they come home at the end of a tough day (or when you come home at the end of a tough day) wants to be subjected to a monologue about your "issues"? This is especially poignant because men tend to be "fixers," and there are some things that a partner can't and shouldn't have to fix. They're your issues, and consequently, your responsibility is to take them to an appropriate arena for resolving. Don't let your past suck the life blood out of your future or current relationship.

The past is a great teacher – if you use your learning and move on. If you don't "get it" the lesson will be repeated until it's learned and it's going to resurface at some highly inconvenient time and bite you hard in the bum. Don't get me wrong, having a partner with whom you can discuss challenges and upsets in your life is really important. However, if you place the burden of solving everything your problems on them, the relationship is unlikely to be one of equals and that, in itself, will become a problem over time.

Feeling cherished, valued and special

Everyone wants to feel like this at least once in their lifetime. We all deserve it. But you must ensure that you choose somebody who has the emotional maturity, stability, capability and willingness for this. And you also have to be prepared to make him feel special too, whenever he needs it. It's about give and take.

Someone to keep me warm at night

Buy a dog! That's precisely what I did in my "gap year" between husbands number two and three, and it worked a treat. Please – get real. A man isn't a bed-warmer. And if you're still scared of the dark, leave a light on.

There are no rights or wrongs, no merits or demerits, in the conclusions you draw from this exercise. What you need and want in a partner is a bit like sex, politics, and religion – it's your private business and nobody else's. These are *your* feelings and your reasons. They're important, valid and valuable. Don't discount or discredit them. Write them down and then park them for now.

Getting to the nitty gritty – empowering yourself with knowledge and troubleshooting misconceptions

Men and women aren't so dissimilar. Obviously, there are physical differences and behavioural norms, but the basics are easy peasy.

1. We all want to be cherished.
2. We want to be understood.
3. We want to be respected.

The gist of all of this is that you may have identified a number of things you would like in your life (or that your vision of your perfect future includes). You may have concluded that these things will fall into place, or are only realisable if you are in a long-term stable relationship. However, that may not be a way to get them at all, and even if it is, it may not be the best way for you.

My purpose in encouraging you to question your motivation isn't intended to put you off; rather it's to encourage you to pause, cool your impulses, and properly reflect upon your relationship mindset. This might result in you gaining a different insight (or two) into what you're really looking for.

One of my coaching clients, Jo, was a 59-year-old high-powered career woman. We applied this process, over several sessions, and by the end of our work together she realised that her feelings of despair about being alone for the rest of her days, were driving her to make very unhealthy partner choices. Jo decided to take some time out of dating, and to just focus on self-care. Nine months later, she contacted me to let me know that she'd met a really nice guy and that they were now an item. It really does work – if you work it!

More food for thought

Let's take stock for a moment. There are many advantages to ripe dating (dating in one's later years). You possess bags of wisdom and have a wealth of life experience to talk about. Having a bit of "relationship previous" makes you a more interesting person. You've (hopefully) developed a sense of humour and you don't take yourself so seriously. In all probability, you're tenacious and you've been around the block which is life, more than a few times. You're also likely to have the willingness to work on yourself – or you wouldn't have read this far. You're up for making compromises and keen to avoid making it a case of "my way or the highway." You appreciate that, inevitably, mature dating will include having to become a good "baggage handler" – plenty on the mechanics of that, anon. This means that you *accept* that when we get to a certain age, we all have baggage of one sort or another, and you learn to embrace it, as opposed to scarpering in the opposite direction, screaming at the top of your voice.

You may have survived trauma and you know better what you do (and don't) want in a partner, and you're more discerning about this. You're more likely to be financially independent, and you don't "need" a man, in the sense that our mothers and grandmothers did. You appreciate that the road to contentment is partially about accepting what *is*, and then finding the courage to change what can be changed.

Your wise status provides you with much more choice and flexibility in most areas of your life. And Goddammit – you're more determined than ever! I hope that you recognise yourself in some of the characteristics I've outlined. If not, please don't worry because we're just at the start of our journey! As we go along, you'll undoubtedly identify those areas where there's room for self-improvement.

Dipping your toes back into the dating pool – reigniting your dating mojo

I know how mind-bogglingly scary it can feel to re-enter the dating pool after a period out. *Nobody* wants to have to do it – but what's the alternative? To sit and wait for Prince Charming to turn up after hours on your office doorstep, and whisk you off your feet? Can you identify the above – the so-called Cinderella Complex

– in yourself? If you can, then I suggest you take another reality check and make old Cinders redundant. These situations occasionally happen – but again you'll know from your working life that, in the main, there's no gain without *'pain'* of some sort – and by that, I mean the effort of effecting change, which is never straightforward.

However, the gain ensuing from this particular discomfort, of re-entering the dating arena, is that you're going to find yourself teleported into a life of emotional enrichment. That's got to be at least as rewarding as finding yourself at the top of the league tables in your chosen profession.

Riva was 39, had never been married and didn't have children. Until her mother's death, she was her mother's full-time carer. Riva was fairly "quirky" and wasn't perhaps conventionally attractive; she admitted somewhat bashfully that she'd never had a proper relationship of any sort.

Riva's image also needed sprucing up, so I referred her to an expert on my IDA panel to help her with this, to boost her confidence. I encouraged Riva to broaden her social network and to proactively ask her friends and family to introduce her to potential partners. At first, Riva was somewhat resistant. However, after some persuasion, she made rapid progress. Within just one month, she met Lawrence, an equally quirky unmarried 40-year-old paramedic, whom she met at an evening class she was taking, on car maintenance. They're now seeing each other on a frequent basis, and are discussing marriage and children. Riva's delighted as she really believed that the opportunity for marriage and children had passed her by.

What's love got to do with it?

Last but not least in this chapter, I'd like you to consider what your definition of love actually is. What does love mean to you? This is really important because many of us have been indoctrinated to confuse love with the acceptance of abuse. As Forrest Gump said, "Love is as love does."

Abuse, whether physical, spiritual or verbal is never love. It's harmful, causes deep, pernicious scars and leaves lasting emotional consequences. Love is respectful, nurturing, life-enhancing and expansive. Never believe that you must love somebody who has or does abuse you in any way.

Please take time out, right now, to reflect and note in your journal what your definition of love is. It's essential to your relationship growth – both with yourself (which is actually the most important relationship of all) – and your significant other. If you have a warped perception of what love is, then you'll inevitably attract sick people, because, fundamentally, you believe you don't deserve better.

WOEs → WOWs (Words of Wisdom)

♥ Be sure you really do want to find a partner.

♥ Finding love is an Inside Job – remember to FLY (First Love Yourself).

♥ Remember the oxygen mask – you can't give from a void.

♥ Practising nurturing self-care is the first step in the journey to relationship fulfilment.

♥ No one else can ever make you feel complete.

♥ Work is a four-letter word – but so is love.

CHAPTER 2

WHAT MEN WANT

Jumping ahead for a moment – in chapter three, you'll have a chance to undertake your own *Wise Woman Relationship Readiness Dating Audit*. For the moment, in order to prepare for coupledom, it's good to know what men want... and it might surprise you. The purpose of this chapter is not a heads-up to act the way you *think* men will want you to act, (you'll get found out sooner or later), or to try to radically change the person you truly are – instead, it's to afford you the opportunity of focusing on developing the positive aspects of your character which already exist, and to work on toning down some of the ones which perhaps won't serve you as well. Arm yourself with the facts and use your transferable, analytical professional skillset to put that knowledge into practice.

Let's hear it from the boys - what they say about women

According to my research and experience, here are the not-so-staggering facts of the matter. Overwhelming, men like women who like men. They value a woman who's a friend, a confidant, and a lover. They're no different from women in that respect. The chasm between both sexes is not as wide as many would like to make out. Men aren't necessarily from Mars nor women from Venus. It's not that black or white.

If we view men as being a totally separate species of the human race, then we invite discrimination and derision. Let's face it – we women hate that when it's applied to us. One of the biggest male/female disparities, and relationship-busters, lies around communication. She says one thing, and he hears something entirely different. I address how to develop great communication skills, in-depth, in a later chapter. The by-product of excellent relationship communication can be nothing short of blissful. Words are extremely powerful weapons and can energise or sabotage a relationship, including the relationship you have with yourself. They should be used with care because once spoken, can't be retracted.

However, for now, suffice it to say that we hear words through our own very personal, often tainted, historical filters, which can include prejudices and faulty expectations.

Men myths versus men facts

With men, a partner isn't *all about looks*, but about different strokes for different folks. That's actually good news, because once you're aware of your erroneous perspective, you have the opportunity to choose a different viewpoint going forward. To believe otherwise (and that the stereotypes are gospel) is to allow yourself to sink into another dangerous morass of a quicksand – that of self-pity. Please don't compare your insides with other people's outsides.

So, here goes, in no particular order of priority, the guys' relationship bucket list:

- **A good listener** – men appreciate women who are just able to listen to them without butting in! Good, tolerant, quality listening is an art, but one which is well worth striving for. This is one of the greatest relationship gifts you can offer to a partner.
- **Spontaneity** – they adore a girl who can just go with the flow when necessary. They love it when she bubbles over with exuberance – but also knows when it's not appropriate to do so.
- **A fulfilled and accomplished woman** – as we previously discussed in chapter one, this is about *being happy as you are* as a person – not about external status symbols. Positivity is a quality which is extremely highly-regarded. What man enjoys the company of a sour puss?
- **A woman who is real** – authenticity is super sexy. If a woman acts in a fake manner, it's only a matter of time before her shallowness is outed. Would you trust a guy whom you sensed was a fraudster?
- **Ready to compromise** – a lady who'll work hard to pitch in, and negotiate in a relationship, so that it's a win/win for both sides.
- **A woman who's funny/who's got a sense of humour** –for sure, life can be challenging, but a woman who can see the funny side of things and who doesn't take herself so seriously, is a winner, as opposed to a whiner.
- **A woman who's caring** – he'll adore you for making him feel valued and cared for. Especially when he's facing tough problems or is feeling below par. Your ability to soothe him won't go unappreciated. Keep him on his toes and surprise him every once and a while, by being extra tender towards him.
- **A woman with a maternal instinct** – when a man's looking for a life partner, of course he wants to be mothered! Why wouldn't he? Are women so different? Don't we always look for our daddies at some level in a relationship – especially if daddy didn't exactly score top marks? Or maybe your "heart doesn't belong to daddy" and of course, if he's looking for you to be the stepmother of his future children, then the prospective mother asset becomes even more important. Even if stepchildren aren't

in the frame, a man will treasure all the nurturing qualities with which women are inherently endowed.

- **A strong woman** – a capable woman who's going to stick with him, come hell or high water. He won't be turned on by someone who throws a hissy fit whenever she breaks a nail or encounters a flat tyre.

- **A woman who takes care of herself** – emotionally as well as physically. Yes – he wants you to look natural, and not to be constantly preening yourself in your compact mirror when you're with him. However, he probably won't take kindly to your traipsing around in a grubby old tracksuit à la Shirley Valentine, with eyebrows that meet in the middle, last night's makeup cascading down your face, and legs with wrap-around hair! A woman who takes good care of herself in all aspects demonstrates that she's confident and self-assured.

- **A woman who's willing to share some of his interests** – this isn't a deal-breaker, but it's relationship-enhancing if you can identify a few interests between you which he enjoys, and vice versa. It doesn't mean he has to get his own way all the time. It's all about willingness and compromise.

- **A woman with whom he can grow old with** – who's supportive, is willing to indulge him in some of his dreams, and with whom he can enjoy a lifelong, mutually loving and respectful journey. Who could ask for more?

What men don't want and assorted date-busters

Guys frequently state, "It ain't what you do, it's the way that you do it." We're all human and liable to make dating blunders, so if you do make one, cut yourself some slack, get out there and just do it differently next time. Life is full of second and subsequent opportunities. The Wise Woman realises that while there's life, there's always hope.

- **Too much, too soon** - you banged on about your "previous" – again this is covered later on in dating etiquette, but they don't want to hear about how abusive your ex was, your life story, or how your daddy wouldn't buy you a bow wow, on the first few dates. Keep schtum for now.

- **You were too keen** – you started talking about your future joint plans. You asked him about his intentions and prospects, or if he wanted to have kids and how many. You interrogated him as if he were in a job interview.

- **He couldn't get a word in edgewise** – you made it all about you and monopolised the conversation. See above re the art of good listening.

- **You got too physical way too soon, and scared the pants off him** – contrary to what many women think, some men do like to be friends before being intimate. Being too quick on the trigger can feel like creeping castration personified. Naomi, a 35-year-old accountant, was out on a first date with a 47-year-old client of mine, Bruno, a lawyer. Suddenly, over the hors d'oeuvres in a Chinese restaurant, she launched herself across the table, attempting to give him a French kiss which would have made the "50 Shades of Grey" protagonists blush. Needless to say, there wasn't a second date.

- **You acted like a slag-off merchant** – you bad-mouthed this one and that one and gave him the strongest suspicion that, if you could do this about others, then you may also stab him in the back. This behaviour says everything about you and nothing about the person you're slagging off. Furthermore, it makes you look like a victim. Nobody wants to date a woman with the mouth of a Belfast fishwife.

- **You behaved as if you were in a business meeting** – a super turn-off! Dating isn't another form of contractual negotiation. As my son-in-law would say, "chill your beans."

- **You complained about almost everything on the date** – this screams 'high maintenance" to a guy and, trust me, he'll flee pronto. There are plenty of other contenders for him to consider, who won't behave like this and who'll appreciate being out on a date with him.

- **You drank way too much and behaved completely inappropriately** – need I elaborate any further?
  Gloria, a 60-year-old retired business manager, drank like a fish during her second date with Ray, a 65-year-old retired dog trainer. Sitting in a busy pub in central London, Gloria whipped out her left boob, in order to show Ray her ex's name boldly tattooed on it, complete with fluorescent skull and crossbones. Ray hightailed it to the gents and was never seen in Gloria's company again.

- **You came across as a drama queen** – you created a storm in a teacup over trivia and may even have enhanced your performance by bursting into tears – simply hideous.

- **The green-eyed monster** – SOS! Too many questions about his past relationships, accompanied by your running commentary on what bitches his previous partners must have been, followed by heavy hints of how you'd never be like that.

- **You're a screamer** – you embarrassed him in the most excruciating of ways by shouting at him in a public place, or speaking at a volume which was way too high for his comfort. Monica, a 41-year-old dentist, was out on a date with Bert, a 44-year-old financial analyst. Within the first half hour, Monica was turning heads – not because of her beauty, but because every time Bert opened his mouth, Monica's hyena pitched, hysterical laugh ricocheted around the bar.

- **You're insecure and indecisive** – whenever he asked you during the date to select an option or make a decision, you replied "whatever you want" or, equally frustrating, "I don't mind." This made you come across as being super-namby-pamby. He actually values input from you on a date as, and when, he asks for it. If he didn't, he wouldn't have bothered consulting you.

- **Humourless** – you sat there all night with a face like a funeral. He felt it was really hard work. Lighten up and enjoy yourself for God's sake!

- **You're a sloppy dater** – you came out on a date looking like a bag lady. Whilst it's true that men value *other* assets a whole lot more than a woman with just a pretty face, how would you feel if the shoe were on the other foot?!

- **You asked when he was going to call you** – Aaagh! And even worse – when you're going to see him again. A turn-off of the highest order, and rated at the top of my very own *Richter Dating Faux Pas Scale*. Harriet, a 33-year-old music teacher, met Rupert, a 36-year-old IT consultant, for a coffee, on their first date. Before Rupert had even reached the car park, following the meeting, Harriet had already called him to invite him to meet her parents at a family barbeque that weekend. Rupert prudently headed for the hills.

- **Texting Tourette's** – no sooner had he dropped you off, did you send him a long, rambling and clearly manipulative text, (i.e. he feels compelled to respond immediately), about what a wonderful time you had? Or were you on your mobile, texting or reading your emails all through the date and weren't present for him. This is horrendously rude.

- **No chemistry** – okay, so it happens. You're as different as chalk and cheese. You can't please everybody. Build a bridge over yourself and get over it. Move on.

In search of dating progress – *not* dating perfection

Remember, you're on a self-empowering – not self-castigating – educational path here. It's not for the faint-hearted. Keep on trucking. It's a case of aiming for progress, and not perfection.

We may beat ourselves up into believing otherwise, but we actually don't have to do anything in life perfectly, nor get it right first time, or even second time, at that. There's no such thing. Perfection is a subjective state of mind which differs from one individual to another. If you keep the spotlight on just yourself, you won't be so self-critical, and end up in compare and despair mode.

Women's dating myths versus dating reality

This section is about removing your opaque dating blinkers. The power to focus on the good men out there, always remains yours, (as does the power to moan and groan about the perceived lack of decent guys). Now, hold that thought for a second. Which makes you feel more empowered? The positive or the negative view? If it's the latter, do you truly possess the courage to change your faulty perspective on men?

You have to be a certain age, look, size, shape or personality type

Let me challenge you to go down your local High Street right now, and look at the evidence that this is a load of old baloney. If you're even a tad open-minded, it surely will smack you in the cynical face that partnerships are a bit like Liquorice Allsorts Sweets. They come in all shapes, sizes, and combinations. You get big people, little people, beautiful people, ugly, fat and thin people and multiple combinations thereof. People present themselves in all races and creeds. There are healthy people and unhealthy people. There is no norm nor is there a standard. And why is this the case? Because *finding The One is an Inside Job*. It's got very little to do with the external façade. Beauty may not last forever, but a beautiful mind never fades.

I've known men who've found profound joy with women who aren't conventionally attractive. I've known men do the same with more mature women. I was married for the third time at 48. My mother-in-law remarried at 81. There's a huge spectrum of what one person finds attractive in the other, and very often it's not externally objectively comprehensible. My own *innamorato* informed me he once had a relationship with a woman who had false teeth, which she deftly removed every night and placed in a glass, before climbing into the sack with him. Another had a gammy leg. Whilst I like to think that the bar wasn't set particularly high by my predecessor sisters, and whilst I also appreciate that I'm not as young and nubile as I used to be, my vignettes demonstrate that the only barrier is your personal filter.

There are no good men out there

The Office for National Statistics has released data which shows that 51% of people in England and Wales are single. The proportion of single people varies little across England, Wales, Scotland and Northern Ireland. So, if you're counting all the people who have never been married, or who are divorced, separated or widowed, as being single, then that has risen above 50% for the first time. That's one hell of a lot of people, so please don't tell me there are no single men out there! Never naively conclude that your ship has sailed.

I'm past it!

Or is the truth more a case of, "I really can't be arsed"? Stop feeling sorry for yourself. Are you generally a lacklustre person in your professional and broader life? I suspect not! You've got plenty for which to be grateful, and living this long is one of the things to be hugely grateful for. Not everybody is that blessed, and we all know people who've checked out of life way too early. Please refrain from transmuting your lush, mid-life status into a whinge, and a symptom of terminal ingratitude.

Men are only after one thing

Yeah, yeah, yeah – and funnily enough – so are some women. Note I said "some." This horrible stereotype is a sweeping generalisation and is yet another, pathetic excuse for staying paralysed and remaining in victim mode.

Men are all bastards

Another contemptible chestnut. Men are not *all* bastards just like women are not *all* bitches. Men don't have the monopoly on appalling behaviour. Women detest being identified with either a *Stepford Wife* at one extreme, or a *vagina dentata*, at the other. Yet many consider themselves to be perfectly entitled to point the finger at men. Bottom line – men are people as are women, and there are good and bad people the world over.

If men have never been in a long-term relationship, there's something wrong with them

If your prospective man still lives with mother at age 55, and there are other pertinent signs, then perhaps this is a case of *Old Father Hubbard* living in his emotional or actual cupboard, and may be a red flag.

By way of a humorous aside, after my second marriage collapsed in my early 40s, I briefly became embroiled in a turbulent on/off episode with a man whose surname *was* Hubbard, and whose elderly mother *did* live with him. You couldn't make it up if you tried.

Perhaps you've never been in a long term relationship either, but is that a strong indicator that there's something terribly wrong with *you?*

Again, you have to judge every case on its individual merits, before reaching any hard and fast conclusions. Why not suck it and see?

I'm overeducated and scare men off

Would you really want to build a future with the male equivalent of a shrinking violet? I doubt it. But in this day of overall male/female equality, I really don't buy this one for a nanosecond. Yes, it's true that some women transfer their work persona into their love life, and I discuss this later. However, no REAL man is going to feel pussy-whipped or intimidated by a strong, confident, successful, sassy woman. There's a vast difference between manifesting self-assuredness and displaying aggression.

The flip-side of this coin could be that you deem yourself as being way too smart for *him*. If you believe this, then I suggest you reserve judgment until you've worked through my *Needs versus Wants* section. For now, give the guy a break.

I'm undereducated and feel less-than

Utter piffle. I come from the generation where many of us women struggled to get ourselves an education because our fathers were stuck in the old ways and possibly even a tad misogynistic. I was forced into taking a secretarial course because my father colluded with a female occupational psychologist who informed him, when I was 14, that I wasn't academic and would probably have no difficulty in being married off young.

Alas, this proved to be hideously prophetic. I developed an enormous chip on my academic shoulder and became solely self-identified by my appearance. Fast forward to 1987, when the horrific death of my son in the car I was driving, and the severe injuries of my daughter jettisoned me out of a miserable first marriage. Subsequently, I took my A levels in 1988 and secured entry to University in 1989, to read law.

I'm 58 and have continued to study and pass numerous exams successfully ever since. I remain up for lifelong learning, big time. If I could pull it off under impossible circumstances way back when, then you can surely do it now, in a time when there are many diverse and better opportunities and such varied modes of study, self-development, and self-reinvention.

I'm not alone in having overwritten my faulty inner academic primary tapes. Others have done the same and now have fabulous careers.

Don't be apathetic; please cross any previous lack of academic achievements off your imaginary obstacle list straight away. As my Uncle Alex told me when I informed him I was going to University, "Si on veut, on peut," (Where there's a will, there's a way). He was actually referring to the analogous experience of seeing a circus elephant walking up a plank, but I got the message.

You've got kids, so nobody will take you on

When I met Peter, I hooked up with a man who had more baggage than a Luton Airport EasyJet luggage carousel during the height of the holiday season. And I didn't exactly bounce into the relationship unencumbered either. Objectively, we were nuts to get together, and the odds were heavily stacked against our staying together, thanks to the external pressures.

Fast forward 15 years, and we're as happy as pigs in s*** – most of the time. The problems haven't gone away, but together we've worked hard, adapted and overcome. Where there's a will, there's a way – but it takes continuous application and perseverance. They tell me that's what being a grown-up is all about.

The point here is that it's a case of "love me, love my dog." Someone who's worthy of your love, will take you on, lock, stock and barrel. And if they don't, they're out on the first strike. You've had a lucky escape.

WOEs → WOWs (Words of Wisdom)

♥ Be real, and be the authentic, wonderful person you are.

♥ Focus on the similarities you share with a potential partner, not the differences.

♥ Be aware of your historical 'perceptions' filter.

♥ Don't buy into myths and stereotypes.

♥ Refuse to practise contempt prior to investigation.

♥ Great love is ongoing work, but incredibly worthwhile.

CHAPTER 3

ARE YOU READY TO START DATING?
THE WISE WOMAN DATING AUDIT

This chapter will help you in two ways.

Firstly, the readiness for dating self-assessment will help you decide if you are ready to get out into the jungle, or if you still need more heart-to-heart (as opposed to hand-to-hand) combat training! Don't worry if you don't get top marks in the audit as the next chapter helps you to improve your scores. The idea of the audit is to help you discover areas you need to consider working on.

Secondly, the Wise Woman Dating Style Spot Check sounds less scary, but the rub here is that you need to get people who know you to tell you how you come across! My experience shows that this is a really valuable exercise as many women have no idea of how they are perceived by others.

Let's start with your readiness for dating. The notion that finding the man of your dreams is just a case of waiting until *Mr Right* wafts into your life and sweeps you off your feet is about as realistic as winning the lottery without buying a ticket.

You *MUST* do the groundwork to succeed.

What's needed is a strident campaign run with focus, boundless energy, and near military precision. The most important part of this is the groundwork. Just as houses built on sand will collapse, couplings founded on idealised mumbo-jumbo will generally last until you find out what he's *really* like, (as opposed to the image you've created of him in your mind), or vice versa. The preparatory work before you get back in the market is probably the toughest, and least exotic, part of the process, but also the most crucial. If you're encumbered by any outmoded, lurking dating delusions, these will only lead to disappointment. Skip this stage at your peril.

Some readers may already be set to begin the search, but others may have to address quite a few issues in their own lives before they can contemplate embarking on a committed relationship with another. View the following exercise as a dating reality check. You'll be doing lots of writing, so have your pen and journal at the ready. This chapter may initially appear to be short in content, in comparison to all the others, but that's because *you're* going to be doing much of the writing. Trust me, if you complete the self-audit with fearless, rigorous honesty, you'll have plenty of insight into your issues, and lots of material to work with.

The self-assessment is divided into three parts:

Part A aims to answer the question: "Do you *really* want to be in a long term relationship?" reinforcing and expanding upon what you may already have gleaned from the first part of Chapter One, "Are you happy being single?"

Part B addresses your emotional readiness.

Part C deals with practical issues.

Answer all the questions, and count how many you answer "yes" to in each section. If you score less than five in any section, I recommend that you read the relevant sections in chapter four – "Essential Preparation" – which offer helpful actions you can take to improve your readiness for a relationship.

Part A – Do you really want to be in a long term relationship?

Assessing your motivation

1. Would you be prepared to move to a different part of the country to be with a new partner?
2. If you're a workaholic, would you be prepared to work less hard?
3. Do you tend to keep busy to ward off loneliness?
4. If you have a great circle of girlfriends, would you be prepared to spend less time with them, bearing in mind that keeping regular contact with your female support network must remain a priority?
5. Are you prepared to risk the fact that your friends might like your partner more than they like you?
6. Could you share your family with a new partner?
7. If your family didn't like your partner, whom would you side with?
8. Are you someone who could let go, and allow another person to take charge of some aspects of your shared life?
9. Are you prepared to risk getting hurt?

Diana, a 53-year-old PA, lived in the middle of nowhere and despite trying very hard to find a suitable partner, felt like she was bashing her head against a brick wall. We worked through the quiz and ascertained that, because her motivation levels were extremely high, she was willing to move to Birmingham to greatly improve her chances of finding love. Within a couple of months, she was regularly going out on dates with a number of prospects and was thoroughly enjoying life.

Part B – Are you emotionally ready?

Assessing your inner readiness

1. Do you believe that you can feel happy and contented, even if you aren't in a long-term relationship?
2. Are you optimistic about your life, definitely a "cup half full" rather than a "cup half empty" person?
3. Do your friends rely on you more than you rely on them?
4. Do you feel physically desirable?
5. How does it feel imagining yourself as part of a couple?
6. Are you good at relaxing and seemingly doing nothing?
7. Do you spend a lot of time with friends?
8. Do you have any health issues which could impact on a relationship?
9. Do you think about a previous partner or husband less than five times a week? If so, answer "yes". You may be divorced, widowed or have re-surfaced after the end of a long-term relationship.
10. In your opinion, are there many men out there who might find your personality attractive, *and,* are you open- minded enough to commit to trying to get to know a man who initially might not appear to fit your list of essential characteristics? Answer "yes" only if *both* these statements are true.
11. Do you feel a sense of vitality and excitement when you think about dating again?

Jennifer, a 38-year-old widow, was really desperate to find a partner. She'd lost her husband only six months previously, very suddenly, and every time she went out on a date, she kept comparing her prospective man to her late husband. Driven by the fear that she'd never have children, she would then lie awake at night sobbing. After assessing her emotional availability, using my diagnostic quiz, it became blatantly obvious that Jennifer just wasn't ready to face the dating world for the moment. Her emotions over the loss of her husband were still far too raw.

Part C – Practical Issues – answer "yes" if these statements are true:

Sorting out your lifestyle

1. Responsibilities for children won't prevent me from dating regularly. (Either you don't have them, or you can arrange for carers).
2. Responsibilities for elderly parents or others won't prevent me from dating regularly. (Either you don't have them, or you can arrange for carers).
3. Work commitments won't prevent me from dating regularly.
4. I can juggle existing hobbies or commitments I've been engaged in for some time, to create space for dating.
5. I can/have set aside enough funds to regularly enjoy quality experiences with a potential partner.
6. I've enough energy at the end of the day to be vibrant in good company.
7. I've my own transport, or live in an area where affordable taxis and/or good public transportation are available.
8. I've no plans to move somewhere which would make dating a person who currently lives close to me, impractical.

Antonia was a 46-year-old partner in a firm of chartered surveyors. She led an incredibly busy life, which we realised was getting in the way of her love life. Antonia filled her life full of activities. Between work, going to the gym, looking after her two teenagers, and caring for elderly parents, she didn't have a minute to spare and was thoroughly exhausted. We discussed various possible solutions and, in the end, Antonia decided to work from home one day a week, for the next six months, so that she could plan her responsibilities around her love life, instead of vice versa. In this way, finding a man was at the top of the list, rather than a hurried afterthought.

So, you've done the quiz. Remember that if you scored less than five, it would be beneficial for you to read the relevant sections in the next chapter.

The Wise Woman Dating Style Spot Check

In order to do a spot check inventory on what your dating style is, it's extremely helpful to seek objective feedback from your trusted nearest and dearest or, if you dare, even from a former partner. You could view it as being like an "exit interview" process, which many more enlightened workplaces adopt when an employee resigns from a job. The input should ideally come from members of both sexes, so you're presented with a more balanced view. These questions are quite personal, but arguably the more surprising the answers, the more you need to know them. Brutal honesty may be painful, but it will also be of greatest benefit.

If the mere suggestion of this causes you to throw your hands up in abject horror, then you must again question your motivation and willingness to go to any lengths to find a life partner. If, after considering this, you're still adamant you don't want to avail yourself of constructive external input, write your responses to the following questions, as candidly as you're able:

- What kind of first impression do they think you make?
- Do they think you have a perceived "type" of man? Does your vision of an ideal man include intractable physical specifics, e.g. he must have blue eyes, dark hair, perfect teeth, etc.
- What do they think is the biggest obstacle to you finding your mate?
- Why do they think you're now single?
- How do they think other people react to your conversation style?
- Do they think your true personality comes across successfully?
- Do they think you manifest any unhelpful and off-putting behaviours?
- Do they consider you in any way "quirky" or "eccentric"?
- Do they think you could improve your appearance and, if so, how?

The point of extracting this information is to empower yourself; to modify and eliminate any unhelpful attitudes and behaviours.

Lucy, a 45-year-old company director, was what I would determine a "damaged dater". She'd been on a seemingly endless series of dates with a load of no-hopers. On the face of it, she appeared to be really sorted but the objective input I received, from her close friends, indicated that she had major issues around trust, which had stemmed from childhood during which she'd been abused by her violent father. Her dating style, therefore, was to unconsciously seek out lousy men because, at a deep level, she believed she didn't deserve any better. Lucy was open to getting professional help from a therapist to work through these issues, before going on any further dates.

WOEs → WOWs (Words of Wisdom)

♥ Make sure you're in the right place in your life, on all levels, before you look for a partner.

♥ Find the courage to seek objective input on your dating style.

♥ Madness is repeating the same thing and expecting different results.

♥ Self-honesty and self-awareness permit you to prise the pearl out of the jaws of previous relationship adversity.

♥ Stay upbeat, positive, and hopeful.

♥ It's never too late to find love.

CHAPTER 4

ESSENTIAL SELF-PREPARATION

Doing *The Work* on yourself

Who's your worst critic? My guess is it's you. I've named my inner dictator Adolf. When the tyrant kicks off, uttering hateful, harsh and staccato commands, I just order Adolf to shut the f*** up.

It takes constant practice to develop mindful awareness of the despot – but it can be done, as I'm committed to working on myself continuously. Despite years of self-reinvention, I still have to keep a sharp lookout for Adolf. He's cunning, and he's powerful, and he can creep up on me at any time. Why don't you give your inner dictator an appropriate name? The more ridiculous the name, the better. It's a light-hearted, simple and effective way to dumb down and eventually silence your inner primary tapes, plus it enables you to take yourself, and life less seriously. In turn, question yourself – where exactly is the evidence to support your wounding diatribe? Where is it written that things simply have to be this way? Why is a particularly dire outcome inevitable? Who, in your past or present, originally chucked this verbal garbage at you? You can go on blaming your parents, your teachers, your former partners until kingdom come, but, although the initial situation wasn't your fault, it's your responsibility and yours alone – to heal yourself now. Awareness is accompanied by the onus of deciding if you're going to accept the status quo, or taking action to improve it.

The buck stops with you.

Liz, a 39-year-old osteopath, grew up with highly emotionally and physically abusive, narcissistic parents. Whatever she did, she could never please them. She spent her entire earlier life, dancing around them, always treading on egg shells. When we met, her parents had died – but it felt like they were still controlling her from beyond the grave. In short, Liz felt like she was merely an extension of her parents – with no separate identity of her own. She found it impossible to silence that super harsh inner critic. The more I tried to convince her that she wasn't a piece of trash and that she did deserve love and happiness, the more she self-harmed, either by spending too much, overeating, or indulging in way too much alcohol and ingesting drugs. It was patently obvious that Liz needed professional, therapeutic help, as her issues ran deep, and were beyond my expertise. To her credit, Liz is now in therapy, working hard on these deep-rooted difficulties. Unless and until these issues are addressed, and resolved, trying to find a nurturing relationship with a man is futile because Liz will merely sabotage it, due to her feelings of extreme unworthiness. First, Liz must learn to truly love herself.

Practising the art of nurturing self-care

Do your utmost to prepare yourself for your re-launch onto the dating scene. Have your hair cut stylishly, check out your style of dressing, and treat yourself to a beauty consultation.

If you're overweight, join a reputable dieting club. There's safety in numbers, and here you'll receive unbridled support and the awesome power of identification with others, who are also on their own weight loss journey. Don't get me wrong, there are lots of men out there who like ladies of all shapes and sizes, but by being healthy and active you will definitely have a bigger pool of "prospects" from which to make a selection and, of course, you'll feel so much better about yourself.

The people you choose to surround yourself with will have a huge effect on your sense of well-being, so please, determine only to hang out with high octane people who energise you, rather than drag you down.

Successful at work but not in love?

If you have or have had a successful career but feel less confident about relationships than you do (or did) about your position in the workplace, can you apply what you already know in your professional life to your love life? I'll wager that you are (or were) dynamic, energetic and focused. Most jobs also require self-discipline and an enormous amount of time and effort into projecting the correct professional persona. You are likely to be, or have been, admired and respected.

These work skills don't belong to your alter ego – they're yours. Take the credit, feel good about yourself, and apply them to the rest of your life - especially your love life. You have to be willing to show dedication to the cause. Why should this be any different or less important than all your hard graft to achieve your professional goals? If you truly believe that your future emotional enrichment is an inferior goal, now is the time to quit.

Susan was an extremely successful 40-year-old insurance broker. When we met for the first time, she gave me her shopping list of her dating requirements. It went something like this. She had to have a man who was available to see her every two weeks, on a Sunday night. He also had to be no older than 40, had to earn far less than her – and had to be willing to be a stay at home husband – in case she wanted to have kids. He also had to live no further than three miles from her home, and have no kids of his own, nor any other family to distract him. Susan gave me chapter and verse on how impossible it was to find a decent man, lamenting on the fact that nobody seemed to match her stringent demands. When I studied the objective input which had been provided to me by her friends, on the initial questionnaire I sent them, the words "high maintenance", "unreasonable", and "inflexible", were glaring at me from the page. Susan had never actually been in a relationship which had lasted longer than two weeks – and this was hardly surprising! Clearly, Susan had an awful lot of inner work to do on herself and – as she wasn't willing to do this, but instead wanted an instant solution to her "problem", I politely declined to work with her. Good luck to Susan – I hope she's found her man, but somehow I doubt it!

In midlife, you must reclaim your 4 "Ps" – your **P**ower, your **P**otential, your **P**assion, and your **P**ersistence.

- Your **P**ower – you've lived a rich life so far, and have no doubt overcome a great deal. Own it and be proud of it.
- Your **P**otential – you've made career choices and have worked for your achievements.
- Your **P**assion – you know by now what floats your boat. Transfer that passion to your love search.
- Your **P**ersistence – you believe that giving in to a victim mentality is a waste of precious energy.

Crashing through your fear threshold

Believing you are going to fail will almost certainly become a self-fulfilling prophecy. The good news is that so is believing you are going to succeed. Of course, change is scary, as is troubleshooting tough emotions. It's very easy to search for the evidence to support your catastrophic thinking, find it, and then do nothing to move your love life onwards and upwards. I want you to transfer the courage and confidence with which you've overcome perceived past hurdles to take affirmative action about your current situation.

How motivated were you to overcome fearsome blocks in your way? Were you prepared to go for it with great gusto? Perhaps you need to seek objective input from somebody who witnessed what you went through. What would your best friend say about you? We can sometimes find it very hard to accept praise and compliments, so next time somebody pays you a compliment – make a note, and refer to it whenever you're down on yourself.

Perhaps you have what I term an APB – an *Automatic Praise Blocker* – which filters out all the good stuff? Too many of us were indoctrinated with the idea that we should shrug off compliments, lest we become big-headed. In absorbing such nonsense, we then set up a lifelong mechanism of denial of our talents, personality, and physical assets, and we focus on our perceived liabilities (as if this self-imposed penance is going to award us some sort of spiritual redemption for bad deeds committed). There's absolutely no need to don a hair shirt, self-flagellate, and exclaim "mea culpa". Why *not* you as a recipient of the good stuff?

Ageing graciously - accentuating your physical assets and increasing self-appreciation

You are so much more than your physical appearance. I intensely dislike the way in which intelligent women are conned into buying pills, potions, and creams - the so-called elixirs of eternal youth. The cosmetics industry is estimated to reach $675 billion by 2020[1]. In turn, $20 billion of hard-earned cash is currently wasted on needless painful and risky plastic surgery each year, not to mention other miscellaneous forms of quackery. It transmits a terrible, damaging message to younger women and it's no surprise that the market is expanding by ~15% per year as we're all told we need to look like film stars. As if all we can look forward to, after hitting 40, are elasticated waistbands and Velcro-fastening shoes.

It's time for mature women to stand up and be counted, and to take issue with such vapid attitudes. We owe it to our daughters and to future generations of pulsating, wise, sizzling womanhood. Self-care is one thing, but self-delusion is quite another.

Amelia, a florist, was 47 when she underwent a double mastectomy. She was petrified of dating – especially as her ex-husband left her immediately after surgery, claiming he couldn't live with a woman who had no breasts! It was tough enough being a cancer survivor, but on top of that, she had to cope with the emotional wounds inflicted on her by her ex-husband. With these most difficult of circumstances as a backdrop, I urged Amelia to focus on really getting to know a guy, to see if she actually liked him, before she told him about her surgery. Her natural instinct was to tell every man she dated, immediately, about what had happened to her – as some kind of disclaimer – to shield her from potential further hurt. This was definitely a situation where mindfulness came into its own, and I taught her some simple breathing exercises to use before and during her dates – especially when she felt the urge coming on, to tell all prematurely.

Bit by bit, Amelia built up her dating confidence, and separated the dating wheat from the chaff, before entrusting her "secret" to a man with whom she felt comfortable getting intimate. Gregg, a 36-year-old journalist, proved to be The One. Together, they worked through all her fears, taking it very slowly and practising mindful communication, and nine months later they were married. This

---

[1] (Research & Markets Report: Global Cosmetics Market 2015-2020, July 2015)

wonderful anecdote demonstrates that a woman need never be defined by her appearance – even in the worst possible circumstances, such as Amelia's.

Creating an age-appropriate "*je ne sais quoi*" for yourself

At every stage of our lives, it's important to keep reinventing ourselves so as to foster further internal growth. I've got a thing about women dying their hair. I'm proud to be a *Silver Vixen* and, the only time I foolishly dyed my erstwhile raven black locks, was before my flamenco-style wedding in 2007. I regretted the experience hugely. I ended up becoming obsessive about my roots growing back in, and then resembled *Geronimo, the American-Indian*, thanks to my two-tone hair. Nowadays, if anybody asks where my roots are, I know they mean Odessa, Minsk, Glasgow and Nice – not a bottle of "Nice 'n Easy".

Tastes vary, naturally, but if you do want to colour your hair, then get expert input and ensure that you don't morph into mutton dressed up as lamb. Have your hair dressed in a flattering style and review your look regularly to keep it fresh and vibrant. You don't want to send some poor unsuspecting chap, into cardiac arrest, when he taps you on the shoulder, mistaking you for a 20-year-old.

If you have the funds, treat yourself to a session or two with a personal shopper or style guru. There are plenty around, and you can ask your friends for a recommendation. If this is beyond your budget, choose the one amongst your friends whose dress sense you most admire and ask them to be your fashion advisor. The chances are they will be flattered by the compliment and will take the responsibility very seriously.

Visit a spa or join a health club. Opt for a fabulous, relaxing, aromatherapeutic massage. You deserve it and investing in yourself like this will provide a high yield, in terms of self-assurance and confidence. You can't take the money with you – a shroud has no pockets – so put your cash into the wisest investment ever... yourself. You'll reap rewarding dividends by making yourself feel good.

Making the most of the menopause and beyond - our mothers' best-kept secrets

This section may not be applicable to you, right now, but the menopause is something to be mindful of. I'm fortunate that I didn't know what to expect, because when it did happen, I went through the menopause from hell. Had I known it was going to be so bad, I'd have hibernated for those atrocious, six gruelling years while I was besieged by it.

My mother informed me that *her* menopause had been a breeze, given that she'd undergone a hysterectomy at 40. Alas, that's not saying much, I realise with the benefit of hindsight, because, frankly, she was always completely unpredictable. Where do you draw the line?

Menopause is a form of bereavement and loss. As such, it has a different impact on different women. You may feel that you resemble a shrivelled-up flower. It signals the end of your fertility, and some women feel that they've lost their precious femininity and are now just an 'it".

If a woman hasn't had children, for whatever reason, she may lament the lost opportunity of being a mother. Others may face the empty nest syndrome simultaneously, which can induce feelings of near panic. Swinging moods, coupled with perimenopausal flooding which, without warning, goes "*whoosh*," to your utter horror and extreme mortification whenever you stand up, are not the best confidence builders as you embark upon a new relationship!

Your hormones may seesaw wildly and you're drenched in a tsunami of hot sweats at the most inappropriate of times. As fresh as a daisy, you*'re not*, that's for sure.

Your nether regions feel like they're as dry as the Sahara desert and your sex life has gone through the floor. Other neighbouring organs can be affected – I was chronically ill and hospitalised with the joys of Interstitial Cystitis. It gave a whole new meaning to the expression, "being bladdered". On top of these other treasures, just for good measure, you may even sprout coarse facial hair, experience thinning of your crowning glory and develop a persistent and seemingly immovable spare tyre, which could rival that of the Michelin Man.

I'm not painting a very positive picture here, am I?

Belinda, a 51-year-old dancer, was out on an embryonic date with Julian, a 53-year-old scientist, and had invited him back to her place for coffee. Whilst they were sitting on her sofa, Julian thought it was a really great idea to ask Belinda what a hot flush felt like, claiming he was enquiring for purely research purposes. Unfortunately, the mere mention of a hot flush triggered a massive one to occur. The expression "sweating like a pig" didn't even begin to touch what poor Belinda was experiencing. The more Julian made romantic overtures to her after making such a crass remark, and the more he touched Belinda, the more her symptoms became exacerbated. The encounter ended somewhat hastily, with Belinda ejecting Julian from her flat, and jumping into a cold shower – not to dampen her ardour, but rather to quell the symptomatic menopausal fire which had overcome her. She found the whole incident, and Julian's manner, completely off-putting and didn't date him again – much to his surprise!

This too shall pass

Take heart. There *is* life after the menopause. If you happen to be one of those poor unfortunates who can identify with the former category of perimenopausal horrors, I'm happy to reassure you that this too shall pass. When you're through it all, the infamous "change" can actually be a change for the better.

You can choose to view it in a positive light. No more periods with all the inconvenience that accompanies them. The risk of pregnancy has also been removed. There's plenty of help available and it's your responsibility to yourself, to seek out and use whatever you need to transit through this dark night of the hormones, into wise, mid-maturity.

I was dead against either ingesting or applying any kind of HRT – until my health got so bad and my mood so low, that I grabbed everything going and my arms, bum and thighs ended up looking like a patchwork blanket, crafted from varying sizes of hormone patches. It took a while to figure out the best combination, but now I'd kill rather than stop taking HRT. It's all about optimising the hormonal balance. Too much and you'll be so gloriously horny, you'll be mounting every door knob in sight. Too little, and you'll spend your transitional perimenopausal days duvet diving, thanks to your low mood and minimal energy levels.

I'm well aware of the supposed health risks associated with HRT. However, there's also the major quality of life issue to consider. You can kick the bucket of anything at any given time. That's the haphazard roll of the dice which is life. HRT can afford you so many health benefits in terms of mood, energy, libido and protection for your bones and skin. Everything carries risks and the net benefits of HRT on the quality of a menopausal woman's life, in my opinion, far outweigh those risks.

I'm not a doctor and it's essential to get advice appropriate to your own personal circumstances. Your GP is your best starting point and, if necessary, they can refer you to a gynaecologist at a menopause clinic. You can also help yourself by eating sensibly, exercising regularly, and generally upping the social ante, so you don't sit at home, brooding over your "loss". Support is available in all its forms, from reading a good book on the subject to joining an online women's forum. But don't allow your self-help book to become merely shelf-help, sitting there gathering dust, in the vain hope of it benefiting you by osmosis. Again – *action is the key.*

The post-menopausal years can be the richest and most productive years of your life. You too could be living so many dreams, as I am. Cherish this precious opportunity for growth and self-renewal.

WOEs → WOWs (Words of Wisdom)

♥ Self-care doesn't equate to selfishness.

♥ Include at least one aspect of committed self-care in your daily routine.

♥ Remember to reclaim your 4 "Ps" – your **P**ower, your **P**otential, your **P**assion and your **P**ersistence.

♥ Make practical arrangements for any care taking obligations and responsibilities you may have regarding relatives (young or old) then go out there and enjoy life.

♥ If you keep repeating the same actions, you'll keep getting the same results.

CHAPTER 5

JUMPING THE ABYSS OF RELATIONSHIP LOSS – COPING WITH TOUGH EMOTIONS

Whilst contemplating the contents of this chapter may not initially grab you as being a cheery prospect, I guarantee that, in order to move forward with your love life, a failure to process the past will come back to haunt you downstream. The sting of your unresolved emotions may well sabotage your hope of current happiness. Please bear with me, therefore, and work through the following, at your own pace.

There are many variations on relationship loss, apart from the obvious physical death of a partner. In addition to that, there's separation, whether you were married or not, and of course, divorce.

The Buddha said that suffering in life is inevitable.

While it's true that all of us, if we live long enough, are going to suffer some kind of personal loss, much as we rail against it, eventually we have to come to a place of acceptance, and then ultimately to move on emotionally. This doesn't mean we ever forget the person we've lost, but that we learn to live with their loss. That knife-twisting pain in your gut eventually does fade.

Nobody enjoys the experience of loss. Depending on the circumstances of this loss, the time it will take to travel and complete the grief journey will vary from individual to individual and there's no right or wrong way to plough through it. It's tough and it wounds us to the core. It may also cause old scars to weep because, even with some emotional recovery time under your belt, there will always be a reminder, a birthday or anniversary, which will apply fresh pressure to that inner scar – a bit like picking at a scab. The more severe the loss, the more those painful feelings may resurface.

The aftermath of loss can sweep you along in an ocean of tricky, unwelcome feelings such as survivor guilt, feelings of betrayal, and sometimes feelings of shame. In some ways, if a partner dies, the break is "cleaner", but if you've been betrayed or left for another, there can be additional difficulties. You may even struggle to retain common friends, so bingo – another loss. You may have had to relinquish your home or move house. Divorce proceedings, no matter how amicable the intention is at the outset, more often than not end up being (at best) extremely tedious and (at worst) a dog fight. They can drag children and other innocent bystanders into legal and custodial processes. Then, there may be financial repercussions.

Dealing with the aftermath of loss

When will it stop hurting? Nobody can answer that. I know that when my son died, I wanted an instant answer as to when I'd stop feeling so dreadful. I too had to learn things the hard way and I soon realised that time, per se, isn't the healer – it's what you *do* with the time that heals. If you choose to sit around ruminating all day, potentially retraumatising yourself in the process, you may well drive yourself into the nearest loony bin. Whilst, of course, there are stages in healing, you simply won't feel better. My life raft was getting into university to do a law degree. But we each have to find our own way.

It can be really helpful to find a source of support to nurse you through the dark days, those endless moments when you wake up with a start to be greeted by the dawn chorus at the "witching hour". Your mind races mercilessly and you dearly wish that your current situation was just a horrendous nightmare. Finding a friend or a relative who's been through a similar type of loss and who's living a full, rounded life again, can be an enormous source of inspiration.

Philippa was a 68-year-old widow who had enjoyed a very happy marriage for 40 years, before losing her husband, the father of her four children, in a tragic accident. She suffered from massive co-dependency issues and believed that she just couldn't function without a man on her arm. For nine months, we worked very hard on getting Philippa to feel good about herself. For a large part of this, I encouraged her to engage in a great deal of self-care and to forget even trying to find a man for the time being. This meant taking baby steps, developing new hobbies, bonding with other mature women in a similar situation, and just getting her to a place where she no longer felt invisible without a man – and, paradoxically, so she felt she didn't need one. Philippa's confidence grew to the point where she booked to go on a ramblers' holiday on her own. She was petrified, but with my encouragement, she felt the fear and did it anyway. On the second day, she met Martin, a 70-year-old widower. Within six months, they were married.

Common pitfalls on the road to healing

You may be petrified of putting yourself at risk of losing a new partner. The very thought of going through anything similar again can be paralysing. But what's the alternative? To end up being an old lady who lives for her cats? Don't you owe it to yourself to have another stab at finding fulfilment? If your partner has died – isn't living a new life *for* them more nurturing of your fragile spirit?

Another difficulty is you may find yourself suffering from "Spare Woman Syndrome" – a perceived threat to your friends who are in a relationship. This can add salt to an existing raw wound. Or, if you've split up from a partner, there will always be the naysayers, spreading their very own brand of doom and gloom, because they themselves are enmeshed in an unhappy relationship and don't have the courage to break free and strike out on their own.

Nor do you need to conform to anybody's stereotypes or expectations. You are you. If you're widowed, then nobody expects you to paint it black permanently, don sack cloth and ashes, and build a shrine to your lost partner. Deifying anybody – be they dead or alive, is a bad idea. If you do this, how could any other real, flesh and blood human being ever live up to your idealised standards? It's not fair on a prospective partner, nor on you! If you do this, you merely exacerbate an already fragile emotional state.

Self-pity is ugly

Self-pity is incredibly unappealing, and it's futile. Unless you find the guts to discard it, it will swallow you up faster than any quick sand. If you look around, you're not special and different.

One way or another, at one time or another, life deals us all a bad hand. Many people undergo major traumas. What separates the wheat from the chaff – is attitude. If you choose to moan about your lot and seize hostages wherever you go, you risk being renamed "Ms Rent-a-Whinge". This is really bad for your self-esteem and your relationship rehabilitation.

Nobody wants to hear what a bastard your ex was. Nor do they want to be treated to a monologue on how saintly your dearly departed was. The bottom line is that most people are way too worried about their own "stuff" to want to absorb any of yours.

How we react to our situation is always our choice. We can empower (or disempower) ourselves, depending on our mindset. This may not be a sexy thought, but I, and many others who have suffered a multitude of loss, know this to be true. If you allow yourself to become totally identified by your loss, you're going to be lonely for a very long time. Your loss IS significant, but it's only a part of you – not the whole story of who you are as a person.

The best way to get over yourself, is to do something for somebody else. Even if doing so only takes your mind off yourself for five minutes, it'll be five minutes less of your self-obsession, which will benefit you and everyone with whom you come into contact.

Later on, I'll guide you through some mini rituals, to help you detox from any past partner loss. For now, I'm running these initial, more general theories by you, as preparation for the action stage, during which we'll exorcise these people from your psyche. So for now – get off the cross of your misery – somebody else needs the wood!

Gemma was a 40-year-old makeup artist, who'd be in a long term relationship with Alan, a 45-year-old restaurant manager. Alan was a serial philanderer and pathological liar. Despite all of his assurances, Gemma kept discovering new signs of his infidelities including, alas, discovering on her 40th birthday, that she'd contracted a sexually transmitted disease, which was the last straw. Gemma's hurt was so deeply entrenched that she found it impossible to go out on a date without giving her companion 'chapter and verse' about how hurt she was about Alan. Not surprisingly, this put everybody off. On my advice, Gemma stopped dating after deciding that her feelings were still just too raw. While she remained in this state, she wasn't going to give any other man a chance. Gemma needed a longer period to recover emotionally.

Women starting over – mindfulness and loss

It's never too late to start again. Ever. While there's life there's hope. While you're breathing – you can start living mindfully *in the now*. Whilst it's true that in every relationship, we *unconsciously* drag every Tom, Dick or Harry into our current zone, mindfulness presents us with enormous self-awareness. Practising mindfulness is a way of anchoring ourselves, right now, this very second, into this day, this hour, this minute.

More importantly, this practice teaches us to 'mind the gap', to provide that split second of choice – that near-sacred pause, during which we can choose to react to stimuli or to respond in a more self-nurturing way. It's cumulative and it leads to the ability to detach from troublesome situations, thereby maintaining our own precious reserves of energy, to be used in a more fruitful manner. How healing is that?

Easy does it – but *do* it

I've already alluded to the fact that the only way out of a difficulty is to go through it. Churchill said, "If you're going through hell, keep going." Take small steps. Set yourself SMART goals – meaning these are **S**pecific, **M**easurable, **A**chievable, **R**ealistic and **T**ime-based. Reward yourself when you achieve these. Remind yourself that you deserve happiness and that you have it within your to recover from (and overcome) any past obstacle.

You can't think your way out of this. You have to take action!

Employ all of the confidence boosters I've mentioned in previous chapters. Grab life and your chance of happiness by the nuts! The saddest words in the English language are "if only". The saddest death of all is a person's loss of hope. Don't let that be your epitaph.

WOEs → WOWs (Words of Wisdom)

♥ Get out of your own head by volunteering to help somebody else.

♥ Continue to write in your journal – it's cathartic. First thing in the morning is best and sets you up for the day.

♥ Dare to trust in life and love again!

♥ Don't compare your journey to anybody else's.

♥ Practise mindfulness whenever you can – anchor yourself to the present using your breath.

♥ List three ways in which your strong Life Force – your wise inner counsel – has got you through difficulty in the past.

♥ Find positive support in your Sisterhood network of healthy friends.

CHAPTER 6

MAKING ROOM FOR ANOTHER PERSON
IN YOUR LIFE

Organising your life

Work, and relationship evasion

Is work one of your major time saboteurs? Do you use it as a hiding place from relationships or a potential source of them? If this appears to be a contradiction in terms, let me explain. You probably work because you have to pay your way through life and you like to enjoy a certain standard of living. That's not a criticism – who wouldn't wish that? – it's a question of applying mindfulness to your work and organising yourself. Otherwise, you risk becoming (adapting the nursery rhyme) "all work and no play makes Jill a dull girl."

Work is a four letter word

Of course, work is a necessary evil for most people – aside from the positives of self-fulfilment and creative satisfaction of course. However, when it becomes your only raison d'être and you find you're missing out on all the things that you've already identified REALLY matter and which you REALLY want – then that's when work can become a dirty word.

Practising excusitis and excuse-busting

When you hide behind your work and use it as an excuse for not pushing yourself out of your emotional and relationship comfort zone. There's security in the familiar even if the latter sucks. Like it or lump it – you're choosing to work so hard that there's no time left for anything else – let alone practising the vital self-nurturing which leads you to mindfully develop self-compassion for yourself and then ultimately leads you to a wonderful relationship with a significant other. Do you recognise any of the following statements?

I'm trying to ascend the corporate ladder, so I have to apply myself 200% to that for now

If you apply yourself to this seemingly noble aim, you'll end up with 400% burnout and the only ascending you'll be doing, will be the steps into the ambulance or up to The Pearly Gates! When does "for now" terminate? For just how long do you want to put off your own happiness? What would you say to your bestie if he or she hid behind this one?

Angélique, a 37-year-old surveyor, was desperate to reach partner status in her firm, by the time she was 40. However, she was also very conflicted as she was also desperate to have children. She kept telling herself that there would be time when she was a partner. In her mind, she had it all worked out. However, her emotions were telling her something else and when we started working together, she was feeling depressed. We worked through her priorities and she decided to shelve her work partnership plans in favour of her life partnership ambitions. The firm could wait – but her biological clock couldn't.

Long hours

No matter how long you work or the late hours you keep, you must keep reminding yourself that you're entitled to a LIFE – and the very best one you can possibly create because – make no mistake – only you have the power to craft the life you desire. I assume that no matter how tough your job is, you haven't completely sold your soul to the devil (although at times it may feel like it) – and you do have some free time. It's down to excellent forward planning to work out what you want to do and when, and then to go for it. It's a case of making use of every opportunity to get the hell out there into the big wide dating world. There are holidays, high days, and holy days, for God's sake. So work them baby, work them! Capitalise on whatever free time you have and make it serve your best relationship interests.

I've worked hard for this

My dears – nobody on this planet is indispensable. Do you think a hundred years from now anybody will give a monkey's because you died with an empty email inbox? If you have any level of seniority, then there's bound to be somebody you can delegate to at work. The art of delegation is a learned skill and if you can't do it – then find somebody who can and model yourself on them. Ask for their help. They'll be flattered and as I keep on saying – asking for help is a sign of strength and not weakness. No man or woman is an island!

I still have to prove myself and my worth

What exactly does this statement mean to you? How do you term your worth and how must you prove it (and to whom)? Your boss, your dearly departed daddy who brainwashed you into thinking you were just a dumb klutz, or are you committing that most heinous of crimes – comparing yourself to your colleagues and despairing? Comparisons are odious and they don't serve you in the least bit!

Are you fearful of losing respect? What about increasing your self-respect, self-esteem, self-validation and personal growth? These objectives are FAR more important than what others think of you. I'll wager that everybody else is far too concerned worrying about themselves and if pushed would admit, "*Frankly my dear, I don't give a damn*"! So if they don't – why the hell should you?

Somebody will nick my place – after all my hard work

If they do, they do; life is full of opportunities waiting to be grabbed by the short and curlies – even if it's not immediately evident. The evidence for this is everywhere. Competing with your peers is exhausting and completely futile. It just doesn't serve you in any way.

A shroud has no pockets

Listen lady – you can't take your cash and your plush penthouse apartment with you. You don't need to earn a fortune to be happy. Quality of life and time well-spent creatively on yourself is so much more important than hitting the next income tax bracket. Again – maybe it's spot-check time so you can conduct another *Needs Versus Wants* analysis. It's my hope that you'll realise from so doing that you can't bloody well have it all, or you may very well end up with 100 percent of nothing – a lonely old woman sitting there, wishing her life away, whose weekly highlight is watching "Corrie" on the box, whilst you sigh self-piteously about what might have been.

Don't you realise that it's much more preferable – and healthy – to exit this life, leaving behind the epitaph, "*Moi, je ne regrette rien?*"

Get off your heavenly haunches/weathered saddle bags and craft a fabulous, self-nurturing life starting from TODAY! You can only be happy when you have a certain amount of money which means you have to work like a dog NOW… but *when* is that magical day or moment? What are your priorities? Your six figure bank balance won't keep you warm at night or inseminate you.

Practising destination addiction – the 'when then' game of happiness

Ah – but you see I can't because I have dependent children, grandchildren or elderly parents who need me, so I don't have time to look for love

Bollocks to this one! Your children will grow up, your grandchildren will survive without you, and your elderly parents will die sooner or later. It's up to you to make whatever arrangements you need to make now so you can have a life NOW.

And there's always a way. Find a babysitter, engage an au pair, go to social services and ask for help for your elderly parents. You simply cannot afford to put your own happiness off. In any case, where's it written that your kids', grandkids', and parents' comfort and happiness is more important than your own?

Elderly parents - breastfed on a toxic diet of guilt and manipulation?

Way too many of us were raised on that most draining of emotions – guilt. Guilt leads to shame and shame leads to self-destruction. We may have been told, that as the girl of the family, it's our responsibility to practise role reversal, and when our parents age then we have to parent THEM. So we put off our happiness and living our own life, because of some misplaced guilt and emotional blackmail.

The fact is – nobody's indispensable. No, not even you! Even with the best parenting in the world at your back, you truly don't have to sacrifice yourself and be a martyr on that cross of guilt. YOU may outlive your parents – and as I did – survive your child. Would you want YOUR kids to feel that they had to put you over and above their own needs and lives? I think not.

If you really can't extricate yourself from the guilt quagmire – despite having made arrangements for your parents' care, then consider going to a therapist for some expert input. No matter how wonderful your folks were à la "Waltons" – it's actually not your responsibility to look after them. Seek help. Share the burden. That's what social services are partly for. Wasted lives won't do you or them any good. Make a bid for freedom now.

Prue, a 58-year-old driving instructor, was an only child, with an extremely toxic mother. When Prue's father died suddenly, Prue's mother became increasingly demanding and childlike, insisting that Prue move back in with her to keep her mother company. Prue conceded and her mother took her hostage – preventing her from going out with her female friends, never mind a prospective partner. Whenever her mother got a sniff of Prue going out on a date, she'd feign an angina attack or threaten to harm herself. Of course, Prue would then stay in and her mother would be as right as rain.

After a couple of months of this cloying emotional castration, Prue realised, with my input, that she couldn't tolerate this any longer. She made it quite clear to her mother that although she was concerned about her well-being, that Prue was entitled to a life of her own, and that if her mother carried on in the same vein, Prue would have no option other than to move out. It was tough at first, and Prue felt consumed by guilt, but she held fast to her fledgling but growing determination. Needless to say, her mother is still well, alive and kicking, and Prue is now happily involved in an evolving relationship with a nurturing man.

Troubleshooting pesky kids

I devote chapter 12, "Become a successful baggage handler", to the thorny issue of dealing with step- and quasi-stepchildren. However, difficulties can also rear their ugly heads with your own offspring – whatever age they may be. Perhaps they've had you all to themselves for years, or they harbour the erroneous and ancient hope that one day you'll be reunited with their father. This feeling is incredibly common and is usually totally out of all proportion to the historical reality. It's important to flag up here that you do have a right to a life! Whilst your kids' well-being and happiness remain paramount, of course, you can't afford to allow them to hijack your love life. Kids of any age should never be given the power to do this.

Nicola, a 44-year-old practice manager, met Andrew, a barrister of the same age. Andrew had two daughters, aged 13 and 14. Andrew's wife had left him for a younger man, and his children had every intention of sabotaging his new relationship with Nicola. Every time Andrew brought Nicola home, his children would be incredibly rude, poke fun at her and generally cause multiple scenes. Andrew didn't want to upset his children and didn't pull them up on this behaviour – despite Nicola's obvious upset. After six months of this relentless "treatment", Nicola decided to give Andrew an ultimatum. Either he kicked his children into touch and set some boundaries, or the relationship was over. Andrew really struggled and decided to go for therapy to help him unravel these complex issues. At the moment, Nicola and Andrew are on a relationship break, but are hopeful of getting back together again in the fullness of time.

Give it a high five – but do reappraise your social life

Are you using a crowded social life as another excuse to avoid getting into an intimate relationship? I'm the first to state that having a really sound circle of friends – especially women – is extremely important. However, there comes a point where you have to prioritise your activities and make your social life work for you, as opposed to against you. Anybody who's a true friend will understand that you have to put yourself first at times. Those who don't – well, you're better off without them, because they'll turn into tangle weed, wrapped around your legs. The bottom line is – that you *can* juggle existing hobbies or commitments to create space for dating – if you want to.

Tiredness – physical versus emotional

If you think you haven't got enough energy at the end of the day to be vibrant in good company, then it's time to up your self-care and downscale your perceived or actual commitments. You only get one kick at the ball. There's a huge difference between emotional and relationship fatigue and genuine tiredness. How many times have you felt too bushed to go out – only to force yourself and then find in a very short time that you're actually invigorated, and have forgotten all about your supposed mental exhaustion?

You don't have to go out on the razz seven days a week, but gradually increase your men-meeting activities. Go through your hobbies with a fine tooth comb and if they don't present you with opportunities to meet guys, then axe them for now. They'll still be waiting for you when you're happily ensconced in a relationship. More on this in chapter eight, "Nifty Networking."

Location, location, location

Are you using your location as another excuse? Unless you live in the back of beyond, everywhere these days has links to where the action is happening. If you have your own transport, or live in an area where affordable taxis and/or good public transportation are available, you really have no excuse! And while we're on the subject of location – at this point, you should also ask yourself if you'd be willing to move somewhere new, where there may be a bigger pool of prospective partners.

Staying motivated – top up regularly

Continue setting SMART goals. Reward yourself along the way in a way that serves you, not potentially destroys you. Have a massage, treat yourself to a facial, eat out with a female friend. Doing all of this mindfully and keeping it in the now, will help to keep you grounded and anxiety-free. Stay positive and don't indulge in catastrophic projection or negative self-talk. Avoid apathetic people like the plague, because negativity will attach itself to you like super glue. Hang out with high energy role models. Remind yourself repeatedly of how far you've come in other areas of your life and ditch that APB – Automatic Praise Blocker.

WOEs → WOWs (Words of Wisdom)

♥ Use your journal to record your progress.

♥ Devise checklists and use your tools.

♥ Make a vision board and put it up where you can see it daily of how you'd like your life to pan out – what would life look like with a Significant Other in it?

♥ Use affirmations until they're coming out of your ears – or at least until you start believing them to be true.

♥ Don't look back – keep moving forward. That's the direction you're going in and the past only serves you if and when you learn from it.

♥ Life isn't a dress rehearsal – we all deserve happiness.

CHAPTER 7

KNOW WHO YOU'RE LOOKING FOR

There's absolutely no point in starting the search for love unless you know who, or what, you are looking for; you are unlikely to find it, and will potentially end up just kissing a pondful of frogs. It's essential to have realistic expectations and remain open-minded about your prospective partner. Be prepared for the fact that you may not even recognise him until you find him!

Your "type" may definitely NOT be your type!

Let me give you an example of what you might think is a dead no-no, from the off. You've definitely decided that you don't want anyone who has "baggage". Oh really? I don't mean to be rude – but we ALL have baggage of one sort or another. This can be physical (e.g. kids and an ex-husband) but is more likely to be emotional. When you're a supposed grown-up, guess what… you're largely governed by an unconscious set of inner patterns and blueprints or behaviour, called repetition compulsions. When you enter a relationship with another, be it a friend or lover, ALL of your previous role models are in the room with you, and unconsciously get projected onto the other person. So, Mother Dearest, Daddy Darling and Uncle Tom Cobley (and the rest) are out to play – whether you like it or not. Does this make you less desirable to the opposite sex? No, it doesn't! Because with mindful self-awareness comes power, freedom of choice and the opportunity to use that knowledge to transform yourself and your relational skills into an enhancing asset, rather than a liability.

As I've said previously, I devote an entire chapter to this in which I urge you to become a skilled "baggage handler". Statistics reveal that we're living in a time when there will soon be more "blended" families than traditional ones (where all kids have the same two parents). It can be done. Many other stepmothers and I bear testament to that. It's not easy by any stretch of the imagination – but does anything worth having in this life, always come easily?

Ascertaining what you *need* – as opposed to what you *think* you need

Now's the moment to get your thinking cap on, big time. It's pen to paper time. If you complete the following exercise with rigorous honesty, it holds the key to your future happiness. And you may find the results surprising!

Needs versus wants

In your journal, I'd like you to make four parallel lists, in four columns.

- **In column one,** make an exhaustive list of absolutely everything you'd like to find in a best friend.
- **In column two,** do the same but list everything you think you want in a partner. Make this list as silly as you like. Spew it all out!
- **In column three,** write down your relationship non-negotiables.
- **In column four,** extrapolate and write down from the above lists what you really, *absolutely,* cannot do without in a partner. These are your true needs or relationship non-negotiables.

Take your time over this. If you've carried this exercise out thoroughly, then you'll have a greatly truncated, far more realistic "shopping" list. Once you've compiled your final list, *highlight it in your journal* because I'll repeatedly ask you to refer to it as we work through the rest of the book. If it's recorded in ink, you'll be far less likely to deviate when you start to prevaricate, justify, or back-slide on what you now know is an essential, integral component on your **Non-Negotiables List.**

The rationale behind the exercise is to demonstrate to you that our personal wants greatly exceed our needs. This comes as a revelation to many people with whom I've used this exercise.

It may also show you that you have MUCH higher expectations for a life partner than for a best friend. You wouldn't put in your best friend list "must have perfect white gnashers like a prize stallion"! Yet we list trivia on our wants list, as I did when I was a strident beardist.

Naomi, a 35-year-old stockbroker, went out on several dates with Harry, a 39-year-old company secretary. Every time we had a session, Naomi presented me with a litany of complaints about Harry. He smoked and drank too much. In fact, en route to their second date, he was so drunk, he fell down an open manhole in the street! He was always broke, despite his good job, which meant that Naomi found herself paying for everything. In addition, Naomi was really keen to have kids, but Harry made it extremely clear, that he detested kids, referring to them as "little bastards" who would impair his freedom. The final cherry on the cake was that Naomi stumbled upon the fact that Harry was in the clutches of a gambling addiction. It was evident that we had to carry out an emergency needs versus wants audit so that Naomi could then draw up her list of negotiables and non-negotiables. What we unearthed was fascinating. It transpired that Harry was very like Naomi's late father, right down to the drinking and gambling issues. Naomi's father had also been a very emotionally absent parent. None of these factors had been in Naomi's conscious mind, but when we had completed this exercise, she was immediately able to spot that Harry had all the traits she didn't want in a partner – and he wasn't even fit material to go on her negotiables list, never mind non-negotiable one. Harry was immediately jettisoned.

The best things come in surprise packages

As previously alluded to, I used to have major prejudices against certain types of men. And I'm not alone in womankind in this respect. By this, inter alia, I refer to facial hair, men who wore vests, and any creature who measured less than 6 foot tall. And bald patches were strictly a no-go zone.

More fool me. I must have passed up so many opportunities with really nice guys because I sported such opaque dating blinkers.

Well, let me tell you that Peter's 5 foot 7, still has sporadic facial fuzz and that I absolutely *adore* his bald patch. In fact, it's become a major asset because I can spot him from the rear of any aircraft on a long haul flight, and, bleary-eyed, can avoid the embarrassment of mistakenly wrapping myself around the startled man in seat 7E, when I return, after a visit to the loo.

Getting honest about yourself and your "prospects"

You have to be realistic. None of us are getting any younger. We should have the maturity to know by mid-lushness that great expectations are merely resentments in construction. They lead to major disappointment. We're not perfect either. We may be a tad weathered by the storms of life. And that's okay and can even prove to be attractive to others because our physical selves have a worldly experience and depth which is personality-enhancing and is projected outwards. Embrace it.

You have to pick your poison

This may sound unpalatable, but you can't have everything. The Santa Claus who dishes out an endless supply of Prince Charmings just doesn't exist. It's far, far more important that you hook up with somebody who embodies all the qualities you value, rather than with a shell of a person who ticks all the boxes in the looks department. How would YOU feel if a guy viewed you in the same way? You'd quite rightly be horrified!

Ella was a 32-year-old sales director with a very stringent working life. She was determined that when she had kids, she wouldn't stay at home for longer than five minutes, as she'd miss the mental stimulation and the adult company of work. Ella insisted on going out with men who had equally demanding professions, and then became upset when she realised that two big jobs in the same household just wouldn't wash. She met Fritz, a 35-year-old electrician, at an open event in her new local gym. They chatted and got on famously and agreed to meet again. However, Ella immediately began to cool off and have second thoughts. She feared Fritz wasn't educated enough. She worried about what her friends would think of her. Ella had been brought up by racist parents who berated "those foreigners". I advised Ella to continue to meet up with Fritz and to manage her expectations, keeping an open mind. I urged her to first and foremost be friends with him and to give him a chance to grow on her. I also told her to keep her own counsel, and not blab about him to anyone, giving them carte blanche to influence her process. A few months down the line, it dawned on her that Fritz ticked most of the non-negotiables on her list and being pretty much a full-time house husband was near the top of his list. Their relationship evolved and, nine months later, Ella and Fritz were married.

Practising contempt prior to investigation

Keep an open mind. The only thing in life which is instant is coffee! Give it time. Don't automatically dismiss a potential partner for trivial reasons. Do refer to your **Needs versus Wants** list regularly, but also be flexible and willing to review your **Non-Negotiables List** to see if your perceptions and needs have shifted in light of your ongoing dating experiences.

Conducting the relationship autopsy

Have you learned from your previous relationship mistakes? Remember – the lesson will be repeated until it's learned, and if you can't benefit from it then perhaps you must experience your painful, salutary lesson until you do. If you're motivated and brave enough, you could enlist the input of a trusted other here, helping you to scrutinise your relationship "previous". The purpose of this is to define your relationship hot spots and identify red alerts. This means that you assess where, and how, your past relationship choices have served you, and flag up negative personality traits and behaviours in previous partners which you may have consciously or unconsciously ignored or overlooked. If you really can't stomach the notion of asking for external input, then have a really honest attempt at answering the following questions yourself, but the autopsy may not serve you as well as it would, had you opted for objective feedback. Remember – write down the answers in your journal – not on your PC!

1. Do you have a particular "type" of man you go for?
2. If the answer to the above is "yes" – list what it is that attracts you to this type.
3. How has it served you to go for this type of man?
4. How has it NOT served you to go for this type of man?
5. List all of the relationships you've had and their duration.
6. Under each relationship heading – write down the three main reasons, in your opinion, why these relationships failed. I assume they've failed or you wouldn't be reading this book!

7. Now be brutally honest – is there a pattern evolving from what you're noting down. List the similarities and differences in each relationship.
8. With the benefit of hindsight – what could you have done to better protect yourself, or indeed done to remove yourself from the relationship altogether, or done to prevent yourself from becoming involved at the outset?
9. What are the lessons you can glean from the above analysis?
10. How willing, committed and motivated are you to choosing a healthier path, next time round?

Undergoing an emotional detox

In order to move on with your life, there are certain rituals you can undertake to help you. But a government health warning – these might appear to be brutal but they are necessary:

- Destroy ALL previous relationship memorabilia. Do NOT keep an iota. If the memory is painful for any reason, then the memorabilia has GOT to go! No keeping it for a rainy day, so that you can drown in a sea of self-pity, whilst sniffing his sweater.
- You're not allowed to mention his name to another living soul. You tell your nearest and dearest friends that you're going to "wash that guy right outta my hair" – and that if you dare to even whisper his lousy name – they've to halt you, presto, and force you to eat your words.
- Places where you've been with him are strictly **verboten**. You've simply no business being there and you may only return there when you've got him completely out of your system – a long time from now!
- Whenever you get the irresistible impulse to surf the net or stalk him on Facebook, you desist from so doing, and you immediately call a female buddy and 'fess up to what you're about to do. You don't need to know what he's doing now nor what the mother of his kids looks like.
- Stop swooning over the perceived "good times" and instead focus on the "bad times". This will prevent you from disappearing into La La Land and self-delusion.
- Do not play music which was meaningful to you both.
- Do not drive past where he lives or works, nor stalk his friends.
- Whenever you feel self-pity, write a gratitude list focusing on all the great reasons this guy is no longer in your life and all the blessings you have, even if you detest your single status.
- In addition to the above – go and volunteer. No excuses! There are so many people who have far worse than you.

Miriam, a 53-year-old osteopath, was emotionally shattered after her 55-year-old husband Bert, a physiotherapist, left Miriam for her supposed best friend. Miriam insisted on locking herself away every night after work and all weekend, listening to what she termed her "suicide music", whilst she got out all her Bert memorabilia, sobbed her heart out, and ruminated over the past – and what she'd done wrong – until the cows came home.

All of her friends were beginning to desert her, as they found her company and her obsessing so draining. It was time to give her a prescription to counteract her debilitating self-pity and carry out an emotional detox. First of all, we destroyed all of her memorabilia. Secondly, I ordered her to come off Facebook, as she was stalking Bert and her former friend. Thirdly, she composed a letter to Bert and to her friend, telling both of them how hurt she was and how badly betrayed she felt. We then burned the letter. Fourthly, I persuaded Miriam to volunteer one evening a week, at a local refuge for women, where she soon realised that, comparatively speaking, her problems were "high class". Miriam gradually began to feel infinitely better, and was able to move on from her painful past marriage, and start dating.

WOEs → WOWs (Words of Wisdom)

♥ Ditch your preconceived ideas about your type of partner.

♥ Your true needs may actually be few, drowned out by your many wants.

♥ Bury your baggage before committing to a new relationship.

♥ Don't expect the impossible from another person.

♥ Remember that your life belongs to you, and you alone.

♥ Every new stage in your life will demand a different version of you – be prepared to do The Work.

PART 2

HOW TO FIND

POTENTIAL PARTNERS

CHAPTER 8

NIFTY NETWORKING

Opportunities to meet potential partners

In the further resources section (at the back of this book) I'll provide you with fuller details and ideas regarding networking for love. But, for now, let me kick start your search with some preliminary tips.

Taking a multifaceted approach to man searching is, by far and away, the most efficient method of finding love. Separating your life into normal activities and looking for partner activities isn't the best approach. You need to revamp your lifestyle in order to create more man-meeting opportunities in your everyday life.

Switching on your EMDAR – Eligible Man Radar

Essentially, you need to switch your **EMDAR (Eligible Man Radar)** on when you leave the house, (which you're now going to do as often as possible, unless you just happen to have a string of eligible men in your front room) – and you're *not* to switch it off until you get home.

My client Alicia, a divorced part-time 40-year-old travel agent with two kids, had a fantastic attitude towards operating her EMDAR. Wherever she went, she "worked" every single opportunity – nearly taking it to hilarious extremes. If she spotted a man she fancied at the frozen vegetable aisle in the supermarket, she'd go up to him and chat with him about the price of peas. When she picked up her kids from school, if she sniffed a single dad at the school gates, she'd be off again and would make overtures to him. Whenever Alicia travelled on public transport, she'd make a point of conversing with all of those around her. She also asked her friends to set her up with men and, because of her optimistic outlook, she had the ability not to take herself or her romantic overtures too seriously. She was soon having a ball and going out on lots of dates. This is precisely the correct approach, which will guarantee results.

Exploring different ways and mechanisms of meeting a suitable man

There is a multitude of ways for finding a partner and you have to exhaust all of them to succeed. Half measures and lukewarm attempts will get you absolutely nowhere. Why not brainstorm ideas with a few willing and close friends? You must be determined from the outset, and believe at gut level, that excuses are futile. You must overcome your own barriers to success by re-programming your faulty inner tapes and the erroneous story you drip feed yourself. The best way of keeping your motivation levels topped up, is by being accountable to someone else, preferably a woman who's already in a committed, fulfilling relationship. That way there's no competition and no axe to grind.

Plan the work and work the plan

As I keep reinforcing, you need to draw up an ongoing campaign plan, and then work it to the best of your ability. The plan has to be constantly reviewed and revised to ascertain what hits the spot and what doesn't. Planning for success in love has got to be at the very top of your to-do list. You have to fit it into your busy life schedule and make it happen.

This involves using more than a little chutzpah; undertake to be your fearless best, transforming your intent into dedicated action. The more you practise something, the more proficient you become at it. The way to build up your chutzpah levels is to do so gradually by setting yourself small challenges. If you overthink about taking a risk and making an approach to a guy, or road testing a different way of searching for one, then you may bottle out of it at the last minute.

Having chutzpah means that you crash through your comfort levels and you keep reminding yourself exactly why you're doing so. Remember – nothing changes if nothing changes. Your previous attempts may not have worked too well, or you wouldn't be reading this book! Remind yourself, ad nauseam, of where you've come from and where you're heading.

The multi-pronged approach

There are several blindingly good reasons for using the multi-pronged approach and, having successfully worked it myself, it's a tried and tested method. The rationale behind it is that if you have several prospects on the go, you won't become overly dependent on the outcome of every date being positive, or leading somewhere. It takes the pressure off you and him. You lighten up, and you actually start to enjoy yourself, which makes you much more likely to be asked out on a subsequent date. It also means that even if it all goes tits up, it's not the end of the world, because you've got other prospects on the remaining prongs. It reduces expectations, and when you've finally found your man and have hit the jackpot, then you can slowly start to wean yourself off the approach in a considered way, over a period of time.

In essence, this is what my client above, Alicia, was doing – operating the multipronged approach. Not everybody is as up for this as Alicia, however. My client Roberta, a 47-year-old nursery assistant was verging on pathological shyness and wasn't at all keen to take my advice. My main concern was that without the practice of doing this, if Roberta did hook up with somebody, she'd take it all far too seriously, prematurely – and would combust her long term goal. In the end, the way I got round it was to encourage her to engage, contemporaneously, in the multipronged approach with another single friend and in this way, they could support one another. In this respect, two proved to be company and not a crowd!

Eating your vegetables and online dating

Engaging in online dating is like eating your vegetables. Everybody hates it, but you absolutely have to do it, because it's good for you! Before you panic, and chuck this book into the nearest bin, let me make it perfectly clear that online dating should be just one part of a wider strategy – not *the* only strategy.

If you set your expectations low and only use this mode of partner search, you may become jaded and disillusioned very quickly. Finding The One is a numbers game and online dating is a great method for this. Whether you like it or not, one out of five relationships now start online. According to research undertaken by eHarmony, couples in the south east (22%), and east of England (20%), are the most likely to have met one another online, whilst those aged 55 to 64 years old, are expected to have the biggest online dating boom, with an expected 30% rise between 2013 and 2030 (to 2.41 million). The fastest expected growth will be in London. I suggest you carry out some pre-online dating research amongst happy couples to inspire you. The more success stories you hear about, and learn from, the more this will enable you to maintain high motivation levels.

Choosing an online site(s)

There are zillions of online sites to choose from. It's entirely up to you which ones you opt for, but before taking the plunge carry out some careful preparatory research. Here are some helpful tips:

1. Refer to your list of negotiables and non-negotiables.
2. From this information, set out your criteria and write them down in your journal. You can devote an entire section of your "dating plan" to online dating. You're going to refer to this a great deal so make it as pretty and as colourful as you wish.
3. Ask your friends of both sexes, which sites they used and which gave them the best results – although do remember that their non-negotiables may vary a great deal from yours. There's no right or wrong here – everyone is on an individual dating odyssey. Among those you consult, speak to people who are still single and to those who are happily encoupled.

Carry out some internet research of your own, searching for reviews of individual sites. Draw up a checklist to help you in your search. Pick a couple of your preferred sites. Don't go on too many at once or you'll end up feeling swamped. It's much better to "work" just one or two and then to reassess as you go along.

Just like everything in life, there are no absolutes about which online site is better than another. Much of it is down to you and your individual likes and dislikes. I can give you some rough guidelines, but it's for you to ascertain the good, the bad and the ugly amongst them. Having already done so much of The Work on yourself, hopefully, by the time you get to this point in the book, you'll already know how to be far more discerning than if you were starting from scratch. Whilst it would be wrong of me to recommend or discredit any specific sites, my advice would be to start with the major tried and tested ones.

Profiles and photos - dos and don'ts

This is super important. I strongly recommend you invest in having fabulous photographs of yourself taken by a professional photographer. This isn't the time to scrimp and save but is a time for appropriate self-investment. Don't be foolhardy. Think of it as applying for a job. You wouldn't write a letter of application on toilet paper, would you? So why do the equivalent with some cheesy snaps from the photo booth at your local Tesco?

And for God's sake smile! The number of online profiles I've seen where the person has a face which resembles a slapped arse leads me to despair. You're not going to your granny's funeral. You want to promote yourself as a fun, upbeat, warm person. Also, choose a neutral background. You don't want to be competing for attention with the backdrop of Niagara Falls!

Before your photo shoot, have your hair done stylishly and practise getting your makeup right. If you can, treat yourself to a professional makeover. It'll pay dividends in return. The whole point here is that you'll feel so damned good about yourself, you'll ooze confidence and this will show and enhance your "pulling power"! Remember that First Love Yourself Principle which underpins the entire book? Ask your bestie for input.

To lie or not to lie, that is the question

I'm all in favour of setting up the True Age Guarantee Movement. By this, I mean that I'm totally against telling porkies about your age. I've encountered this situation repeatedly. You may retort that everybody lies online, but that just doesn't hold water. Just because some may be doing so, it doesn't mean that you have to sink to those depths too.

I think it's appalling to embark on a relationship, telling porkies. First of all, you'll eventually get found out, and end up with a big, fat well-deserved dollop of egg all over your chops. Secondly, you're beginning what you hope will be a lifelong relationship, with foundations built on sand. Being a certain age is nothing to be ashamed of. The number in itself is meaningless anyway. You're more than a number so why be ashamed of it and risk discovery? If you lie, what does that say about your levels of integrity? It's a really bad footing to get your relationship off on.

And how would YOU feel if the guy lied about such an important issue to you? It's just not worth the hassle and grief. Don't be a copycat and fall off the metaphoric cliff, like a lemming, just because everyone else is doing it! In fact, don't lie about any aspect of your life.

If ever the "don't lie" maxim was reinforced, it's in the following anecdote I once encountered, in a different work capacity, with a 50-year-old TV executive called Lamorna. Feeling completely washed-up and washed-out following an extremely acrimonious divorce, Lamorna went to Senegal for two weeks, to "find herself". An excitable, sex-starved fledgeling cougar-in-training, she soon found herself doing a very enjoyable line with Abdul, the local medicine man. Abdul was an extremely handsome, 21-year-old Senegalese. Alas, Lamorna did NOT find her Prince Charming in the swarthy, testosterone-fuelled, muscle-rippling Abdul. After a tearful departure, promising to return to marry Abdul as soon as possible, she immediately found herself landing in boiling hot water when burdened with an unknown "gift" to take home to Abdul's "friend" Mohammed, in Glasgow. Lamorna was abruptly halted by HM Customs at Glasgow airport, where large quantities of another sort of "line" were discovered concealed in her luggage (cocaine). Lamorna is now banged up inside the salubrious walls of Glasgow's Barlinnie prison, serving a 10-year sentence for drug smuggling. Needless to say, she never heard from Abdul again. When she periodically used to write to me from the clink, pleading for clemency from me, gushing self-piteously, *"but Abdul told me he loved me, that he'd never felt like this about anyone before"*, I had to restrain myself from catching the next flight to Glasgow, in order to personally deliver a resounding slap across her naïve, trusting chops.

Investing in professional help to draft your online profile

If you feel that your writing skills aren't the best, then it's money well-spent to engage an appropriate person to draft your profile. I offer this service to my own clients. This is your principle online marketing tool, and you need to pitch yourself in the most effective manner. We all judge people by first impressions (like it or not) and nowhere is this more the case than online when you're at least initially interacting with a stranger. Or you could ask a good friend – male or female – to help you out; preferably one who's already engaged in online dating (and is in a relationship) but not one whom you feel might have some sort of axe to grind, which could affect their objectivity!

You must present your assets online, to the best of your ability. Your profile should be succinct, informative, witty, and leave your prospect gagging to meet you to find out more about you. You're not writing a salacious autobiography – your profile should be what's termed in marketing speak as being "a delighter" - an enticement to take the next step – whetting the appetite of your prospect.

Getting "Le Look" right

Let's not beat around the bush. You want to look feminine so wear something that makes you feel this way. This isn't the time to wear your Shirley Valentine 100-year-old tracksuit or the boiler suit you wear when you're overhauling your car. Wear something that flatters your figure and is just a tad sexy. I don't mean you should wear your most effective Gossard Wonderbra (oh boy, am I showing my vintage), so that your knockers are the first thing your prospect sees. There's plenty of time to "flash 'em" at him, further downstream. I mean I'd like you to wear something which is just a tad alluring.

I once coached a 39-year-old classic car dealer, called Nigel. He was extremely attractive and affable, but his lament was that whenever he went out with a woman of a particular type, she'd spend most of the evening looking at herself in her powder compact, preening herself, and reapplying her lipstick. It's surprising how many times I've heard guys say this. Ladies beware!

Practising safe online dating

This should be like practising safe sex – you must go at your own pace. Here are some practicalities to help you on the first few dates. I've already covered dating styles in a previous chapter, so what follows below is purely about keeping yourself safe:

- Meet and remain in a public place, until you feel comfortable enough in the future, with your date, to meet elsewhere.
- Keep the first meeting brief – if it goes well you can meet again! So coffee shops, a bar, an art gallery, etc.
- Tell someone where you're going and arrange to check-in with them when you get home. Don't forget to do this or you may find a search party turning up on your doorstep!
- If you feel ill at ease and that there's something wrong – you can call a halt to proceedings at any time you like. Trust your instincts. You have them for a reason, and you don't need to explain yourself to your date.

- If you're super nervous, you could ask a friend to call you during the date, and you can then pop out for a quick breather.

Mindful networking

In order to ultimately seize the guy – you have to seize the day and any and all opportunities to meet him! Men are to be found everywhere and anywhere, even though you may initially deny it vehemently.

Your best friend may have a brother. He'll have friends. You go to the supermarket – karumba – behind the frozen vegetable aisle you may meet your guy, like Alicia. You have to be constantly on the lookout – like a submarine with a man-hunting periscope.

Maybe this doesn't feel "natural" to you, but neither is spending the rest of your life alone! Trust me – the more you practise it, the better you'll get at generating opportunities. Your future happiness depends on it. This is where you must transfer your professional networking skill set to networking for love. You don't need anyone's permission, you've just got to do it fearlessly. I'm not saying that you should appear desperate or mimic the lead character's best friend in the film "P.S. I love you" (who's single and desperate, and on approaching men, asks them: "Are you single? Are you gay? Do you have a job?"). Don't be pushy but do be proactive.

Using your professional network

There's absolutely no reason why you shouldn't also use your professional network to meet a man. Yes, it's important to be discreet, to maintain your dignity, and to protect your reputation, but I'd always advocate that you do this anyway. Plenty of people meet through work, so why the hell not you as well? I'm not encouraging you to get legless and shag your boss over the photocopier at the next Christmas party, but you get my drift! Have no shame about networking in this way – you'd do it for a job! No need to be pedestrian about your love search, therefore, and shun this as a means to an end.

Interest groups

Whatever tickles your fancy amongst your current interests and hobbies can be transmuted into a man-meeting opportunity. That is, unless it's something like knitting for beginners, or belly dancing. Having said that, Peter can knit – so you just never know! And – following on from my previous advice, remember the Six Degrees of Separation theory. This is the idea that all living things and everything else in the world are six or fewer steps away from each other so that a chain of "friend of a friend" statements can be made to connect any two people in a maximum of six steps. So your pal at the sewing bee could hold the key to your future success in love. As always, you must adopt a sanguine approach. Mealy-mouthed excuses won't wash.

Of course, you can maximise your chances of meeting men by undertaking some research and signing up for man-friendly evening classes in car maintenance, darts for beginners or archery, to name but a few! Use your imagination, and generate your own man-meeting ideas, using the wonders of the internet (it's the best dating aid you could ever have).

Holidays

You can embark on a normal holiday – or you can hook up with an organisation which organises holidays for single people. When I owned Dinner Dates, we organised several holidays every year, in the UK, and further afield. Some of these were special interest holidays, like skiing, and others were for people with more general interests. Going with a singles organisation provides you with safety in numbers.

And don't scoff! My widowed mother-in-law, aged 80, met her second husband on a cruise – and married him six months later. It didn't turn out to be a shipboard romance after all!

Dating events

At Dinner Dates, we held two events a week, which were hosted by our team. We organised various types of social gatherings, in first-class venues, with dinner and drinks parties. Hosting enabled our guests to feel far less nervous as we generally made the introductions. We then followed up (after the event) with a feedback call. It was our policy that for most of these events, we had equal numbers of men and women. We found that even if people didn't find the love of their lives at our events – which actually many did – they made new friends of both sexes, so there's really no downside to going along to similar sorts of dating occasions. Again, I include some of these organisations in the resources section.

Introduction agencies and bureaux

These are organisations to which you pay a fee and they try to find a match for you, depending on your criteria. This is very helpful for people who are incredibly busy, but the service doesn't come cheap. Like everything else, there are reputable and disreputable ones. Signing up with one of these is best done on a recommendation from somebody who's had a successful outcome to their membership.

Speed dating

Personally, I don't like speed dating. I feel that it only affords you the opportunity of obtaining a snapshot of someone in a very short space of time, and this may give you a wrong impression, leading you to disregard the person as a prospect. I also believe it plays right into the hands of the shallow world we live in, where people are judged by their looks. There's so much more to a person than their appearance!

On the positive side, speed dating does allow you to rack up the experiences of chatting to people and having a bit of fun, so if this appeals to you, then give it a whirl, but keep your expectations low.

The meat market syndrome

Once you get past a certain age – and for me, that was in my early thirties – picking up men in bars and clubs can make you feel like you're just one of many cattle up for grabs in a meat market. The sense of competition can feel excruciating and can buy straight into your "compare and despair" issues. You begin to view other perceived lithe young things as being more "successful" in the stakes than you. I'd never advocate that you venture down this route unless you feel totally comfortable about putting yourself in such a potentially demoralising environment. The negatives outweigh the positives unless you just want a laugh and a night out with the girls.

Topping up your motivation levels

I swear by the power of using visualisation techniques, as well as creating vision boards. With visualisation, you actually see the outcome of your desires and act as if it's happening right now. You don't allow doubt to creep in and you keep all your statements positive. It's not a million miles away from practising meditation, where you maintain your focus on one thing for a period of time.

Vision boards are created using photographs, drawings and statements of what you want to achieve in the future. So, for example, you could have a picture of a happy couple, or a wedding. You position these vision boards wherever you're going to notice them on a daily basis, and you commit to reviewing them when you feel your courage waning.

Both visualisation and vision boards go in tandem with affirmations, which I've previously mentioned. Think of writing down affirmations by hand as being the opposite of having to write lines when you're naughty at school! They're positive and eventually become a part of your inner fibre if you use them properly. They help you to project confidence, even if internally you're actually faking it to make it.

Listening to rousing music, and bopping around the house, does it for me every time I feel my mood slipping. Once you find a method which works for you, *use it frequently*.

Ongoing self-assessment

Assessing your progress and results will help you maintain your mojo. Keep meaningful records by recording all your activities and dating outcomes in your journal. You might even want to create a graph, plotting your future and defining where you currently are on your love journey.

Two's company, but three can be a crowd – dating inhibitors

You may feel a lot happier and a bit more confident if you go out and about searching for love with a friend who's also on the same mission. However, while this may boost your wobbly confidence initially, there are also downsides to employing this particular mechanism.

Suppose you both fancy the same guy. Or what if the guy **YOU** fancy has taken a shine to your pal? Is this going to develop into a case of "handbags at dawn", feuding over said chap? Can your friendship survive the fact that one of you may get lucky, whilst the other one is left feeling like the fifth wheel of a car?

It's entirely up to you and I only suggest this for fledgeling return daters, because of the risks and misgivings. Ultimately, only you can weigh it up and decide which path to follow.

Help is the sunny side of control

You must learn to stick with the winners in love and not the whingers; you should ignore unhelpful input from others. Some of your so-called friends may have their own personal agendas. When you're in the company of your friends, a helpful barometer to ascertain whether they're energisers or drains, is to ask yourself how do they leave you feeling after you spend time in their company? It's useful to compile a written record of people who raise your spirits; put all the energisers on your A list. All others go on the B list and you either minimise contact with them, or you cut them right off. Life is tough enough. You owe it to yourself to conserve your precious energy, which is best spent elsewhere on nurturing and empowering activity rather than wasting it on losers. You don't ever have to explain your reasons why.

Listen to, and trust, your gut. Your intuition was given to you for a reason and we can easily drift into the malaise of overthinking and rationalisation which leads straight into the false safety of inactivity.

WOEs → WOWs (Words of Wisdom)

♥ Love is a verb – without action, it's merely a word.

♥ Keep your dating cool and fast-track your confidence.

♥ Always put your physical, emotional, and financial safety first, whatever method of dating you engage in.

♥ I'm not asking you to become Mother Teresa – but don't frigging lie!

♥ Kick love saboteurs into touch.

♥ Don't seek everyone's opinion – trust your instincts.

CHAPTER 9

MAKING AND INSTIGATING CONTACT IN THE EMBRYONIC STAGES OF A RELATIONSHIP

Connecting with someone in a social context

Scan the room discreetly to ascertain whom you'd like to meet. Turn down the volume on any inner chattering doubts and turn up your confidence volume. Approach the person and smile at him. If he's mid-conversation, don't interrupt, but wait for a convenient pause. You have to put yourself in his path to flirt, but don't seem too obvious.

Getting a conversation going at any social event

Introduce yourself and then create the opportunity to chat about something you have in common. You can unearth this by asking him open questions – e.g., "how do you know our host?", "what do you do?", "where have you travelled from tonight?", "what did you do at the weekend?", "what sort of a day have you had today?" Once you find your initial "hook" in the opening conversation, you should be able to establish a dialogue flow thereafter.

Show your interest in him

Encourage him to talk about himself as much as possible. Find out what he's passionate about, and get him chatting about this. Ask open questions so he can't just answer "yes" or "no". Be a great listener – don't interrupt and use his name when you can. Don't talk about yourself non-stop.

Body language

Draw attention to your body by wearing something which is feminine, vaguely provocative, and which leaves him guessing. Accentuate your body's assets and forget about those body "liabilities"! Head up, shoulders back – and smile! Lots.

Smiling makes you seem attractive. Flip your hair. This is SO feminine!

Crash through the touch stigma. Find ways to lightly touch him when you can. If he cracks a joke, let your hand rest on his forearm while you're laughing. Touch his shoulder lightly. Establish a sense of fun and camaraderie with him. Lean towards him whilst talking to him. Never cross your arms as it makes you appear to be defensive. Make him feel he's the most special guy in the world by giving him your full attention and keep looking him straight in the eye. Don't allow yourself to be distracted. Laugh at his jokes – even if they're terrible! Ask him to dance and then let your inner goddess come to the fore – but in moderation. Dancing's a great way to connect with a man in a flirtatious way.

Rochelle, a 37-year-old landscape designer, reported back to me that, at a close friend's recent party, she'd tried to connect with several men whom she found attractive. Rochelle gave me chapter and verse about how awful it was and how my advice just hadn't worked. I suggested that she speak to her friend, whose party she'd been at (for feedback), and the next time we met, Rochelle sheepishly admitted that her friend had informed her that Rochelle had gone into overkill and had virtually chased the men around the room, trying to engage them in conversation. It's all about balance – and practice!

Be playful

Tease him gently about minor things – it shows him that you're fun and have a sense of humour. Find something you admire about him and pay him a few compliments. Everyone enjoys having their ego massaged! Don't go overboard though. Expect to be teased back! It'll show him you're a good sport. Keep the conversation light – no relationship post-mortems on your side or grilling him about his ex. Best also keep off the thorny topics of sex, politics and religion – for now anyway!

Leave him wanting more

Don't exhaust the conversation to the point that there's nothing more to chat about. Walk away while he's still interested so he realises he must see you again. Leave an opening for "a next time". Say you have to dash off now, but maybe you could get together sometime soon to continue the conversation? If he says "yes", ask for his contact details.

Men like women who are proactive. Why should they make all the running? Don't act too desperate as this will be off-putting. Listen to your intuition and trust your instincts – he's not the last man in the world you'll meet, so if he doesn't take the bait – don't panic. It's his loss. There are plenty more fish in the sea! Remember to read his body language. If he's backing away so fast from you that you start to fear you have a catastrophic dose of halitosis, then take it as read that you need to move on to somebody else!

Fear of rejection

Look – man, woman, beast, fish or fowl – we ALL want to be loved. Nobody likes being rejected. It hurts like hell and very probably brings up a load of really unhelpful stuff from childhood, which just doesn't serve the adult you. However, it's there, and it would be remiss of me not to give you advice on how to soften the blow. Our subconscious mind can throw us a mental stink bomb and sabotage our chances of finding love again now or in the future. Here, therefore, are some suggestions to foster damage limitation.

- **You're not being rejected as a person in your entirety.** Your prospect just doesn't want to get into a relationship with you for whatever reasons of their own. This is actually a positive if you can reframe the situation because they're doing you a favour. Why would you want to get into a relationship with somebody who's only lukewarm? It would only end in tears downstream – yours! You deserve The Real Deal – and you'll find it – if you pick yourself up, dust yourself down and start all over again.

- **There's never just one person for you in the universe.** If ever there was proof of that, look at my situation. I'm now happily married, but it took me three attempts to find Mr Right! Did I give up? No I did NOT and the night I met Peter, I knew instinctively that if I didn't do anything to engineer meeting him again, I'd miss my Big Chance of love. So I went after him – and the rest is history! More on that anon. I've had more than my fair share of rejections – which at times felt as pleasant as a dog cocking its leg for a piss against a tree! I got over them, adapted and kept going – and you can too.

- **Brainstorming.** In your journal, write down all the times you've succeeded in reaching tangible goals in every area of your life. Include school, university or college, work, giving up smoking, losing weight, taking up a new activity, and so on. This activity is intended to boost your self-confidence and to sharply remind you that you're a great person with great worth.

- **Reflect on past "failures".** The point of dwelling very briefly on your past mishaps is so that it dawns on you (PDQ) that you have actually survived rejection and perceived failures. I bet you struggle to even list these in your journal! I suggest that you start a section in your journal called "overcoming failures". This is actually a positive move, because perceived failures can turn out to be your best learning experiences, *if* you choose to learn from them!

- **Keep it in the present.** Whilst it is useful to think of past rejections, this is only intended as a very brief exercise and not an excuse to wallow! This also involves wising up to the fact that, as so much of our reactions are fuelled by the subconscious, we must remember that we're actually living in the NOW – which is the only time we have. So, even though your subconscious may attempt to sabotage you today by making you feel that you're being rejected or punished by your parents, school teachers and previous partners – I'm here to tell you that the past is no longer relevant! Carrying out mini rituals, to expunge your painful memories of past negative events, can be very helpful. You could burn memorabilia, such as photographs, related to that period of time. Or you could write the most foul swear words all over pages in your journal, and then rip those pages up. You have the opportunity to be mindful and seize the moment; unearth those subconscious feelings, spew them out on paper, and choose to react differently in the present. You don't need to overload the present with the shit of the past. You really don't! It may not feel that you've a choice – but you truly, really do. You've the power of choice which lies in the moment, not the past.

- **Refer to role models and mentors.** Look around you and consider the fact that anyone who's achieved jack shit, will have also endured rejection – and not died from it. Speak to a buddy, read about an inspirational person. In all areas of life, you'll find folk who've been rejected in every sphere. They survived it and prospered and so will you.

- **The beauty of practising The Multipronged Approach.** I've already referred to this in a previous chapter. The fantastic byproduct of practising this, is that if you've got several prospects in the frame, then the sting of rejection will hurt one hell of a lot less, because you'll still have plenty of options! Just visualise a fishing rod with lots of hooks on the end of it, with worms wriggling furiously, waiting to be used as bait. I dare you NOT to lighten up and feel less sorry for yourself after you've conjured up this mental image!

Asking for contact details

Okay, so having gotten over the hump of your fear of rejection, how do you move matters onto the next level? In this day and age, there's absolutely nothing wrong with your taking the bull by the horns and asking a guy for his contact details and then making contact. If you're not prepared to do this, then you shouldn't be reading this book! It's not "unromantic" or aggressive or pushy. If your gut instinct is that you've made a connection with somebody (and I can't tell you that, only you can sense it) – take the plunge!

Arabella, a 45-year-old vet, was incredibly shy and the thought of asking a man for his contact details caused her to nearly freak out. Not all clients enjoy the process but, in this situation, I often find that doing a short pre-date or event role play (with me) can help ease the trauma of actually doing the real thing with a potential new partner. We did role plays over several sessions and Arabella found that the more she practised this new skill, the less anxious she felt about doing it.

Ways of taking the proverbial by the horns

- At the end of your first meeting – ask him! Offer to give him your contact details and ask for his.
- If you've been listening properly to him during your first meeting, you'll have gleaned valuable information about his interests. Suggest you meet up to engage in one of these – if you're indeed interested. I'm not saying you should suddenly pretend to be into kick boxing, if you're not, because you'll only end being shown up as a fraud, and risk getting a Frank Bruno nose in the process!
- Wait a few days then send him a very short text or email, saying how much you enjoyed meeting him and suggesting putting a date in the diary in a few weeks' time to go for a drink, see a movie, go for a walk or meet for coffee. Dinner at this embryonic stage is too much. See how it goes in small, bite-sized stages.

What NOT to do

- Stalk him!
- Phone him and hang up just so you can hear his voice.
- "Just happen to be" in the same location as him at the same time.
- Interrogate his friends.
- Start practising writing your first name with his surname!
- Blabbing to everyone including posting it on Facebook, that you've met Mr Wonderful and will soon be an item. For God's sake keep your powder dry for now.

Look for the similarities and not the differences

When you meet somebody you might be interested in, it's vital that in your very first encounter with them, you look for communal similarities between you *and not the differences*. For at least now, if you focus on the former, this will give you plenty of opportunities to see if you're actually a possible relationship fit; enough to get the ball rolling. It's absolutely crucial to maintain that open mind and not shut any doors and – if you don't try, you don't get – and you may miss a great opportunity. Don't give your fears and doubts fertile ground to spread, like pernicious weeds, before you've even given yourself – and him – a chance for exploration of mutual possibilities!

Marla, a 60-year-old retired psychotherapist, couldn't stop herself from dragging her past work experience into every encounter with a man. She'd go into hyper-analysis mode and dissect everything the poor guy said, finding hidden meanings and issues which clearly didn't exist. I realised, after a number of near-misses, that Marla was actually using this as a defence mechanism, to protect herself because she felt anxious. By always focusing on a guy's perceived negatives, she was keeping herself at a safe distance, thereby protecting herself. Once she became more mindful of this, she began to relax, and a whole new dating world opened up for her.

WOEs → WOWs (Words of Wisdom)

♥ Be proactive – men don't have to make the first approach.

♥ Don't take a perceived rejection personally.

♥ There's no such thing as failure – just a learning experience. We only fail when we stop trying.

♥ Take it one date at a time.

♥ Neither jump the gun – nor the guy – too soon by publicly declaring yourself as an item.

♥ Enjoy the process and persevere.

CHAPTER 10

SPOTTING AND EXTERMINATING YOUR INTERNAL SABOTEUR AND THE IMPOSTOR MENTALITY

Vanquish the victim mentality

By now you'll have no doubt got the message, loud and clear, about The Inside Job Principle, and how vital it is to do the Inner Work before you go out there searching for a partner.

This entire chapter, however, is dedicated to an issue which plagues so many women – that of their hideously powerful false internal voice which I call *The Saboteur*. It bellows at us like a foghorn in search of the Titanic. And what it says sure ain't pretty. It can undermine you in every area of your life – and most potently with your love life.

The Saboteur is that pernicious internal voice, which unconsciously compels you to screw up each and every good opportunity that comes your way.

The corrosive toxin of chronically low self-esteem and The Impostor Syndrome

As I write, we've just celebrated International Women's Day 2017. But in the cold light of day, how equal do we *really* feel? In theory, we're equal in all ways to men and there are discrimination laws in place. In practice, prejudice and ignorance are, sadly, still rife. I've battled with this all of my life and still have to keep tabs on it.

One consequence of prejudice and ignorance is what I call *The Impostor Syndrome*. It's the relentless, self-castigating tape, which informs you that you're a fraud, in pretty much any area of your life, and that it's only a matter of time before everybody else discovers this heinous fact. When I got into law school, I found out that my fellow female students also suffered from it which was in some ways a welcome surprise, because then I felt I was no longer alone with this particular aspect of my personal struggle. The Impostor Syndrome and The Saboteur are inextricably linked, the first often leads to the second. If you don't stamp on your

Impostor Syndrome, it will dog you across all areas of your life, and like an unpredictable, vicious mutt, will leap up and bite you hard on the arse. It will tell you that you're not good enough, and it will ensure that your worst predictions come true.

Nowhere is this truer than when you seek a relationship. First of all, you may believe that there are no decent guys out there. Then, if and when you find a good 'un, you may spend YEARS nearly sabotaging your relationship, because your primary tapes keep screaming at you that you're unworthy and don't deserve this relationship and this great guy. So, in all sorts of pernicious, subtle ways, the relationship begins to fall apart – and your catastrophic thinking becomes a self-fulfilling prophecy. You end up in a heap, further castigating yourself and beating the hell out of yourself with "I told you so".

You may then gravitate to other doom and gloom merchants, and sit round in a circle like a coven of witches, kvetching about how shit men are. But actually – fundamentally, the buck stops with you! YOU are choosing to sabotage YOUR chances by either repeatedly hooking up with the wrong guys – or telling yourself you're not worthy of the love of a decent guy.

When there's a disconnect between what you know in your head to be true and what you feel – erroneously – then you're suffering from a nasty case of The Impostor Syndrome.

Miranda, an extremely attractive 38-year-old lawyer, fought a lifelong battle with her low self-esteem. She'd been brought up by extremely narcissistic parents and had further abuse heaped on her at the convent boarding school she attended. Miranda was repeatedly verbally and physically trashed and, of course, had bought into various myths, which were destroying most of the aspects of her life, including her love life.

I instructed Miranda to write a daily gratitude list, every morning, with five different things she appreciated and liked about herself. I also instructed her that these five things had to be different every day – so no repetition. Her task was to then review this list nightly before she went to sleep. Miranda nearly baulked at the prospect, but to her credit showed willing, and a very subtle and slow transformation began to take place in her feelings about herself.

You've got The Power

You really do! Perhaps you grew up in a family, as did I, with three older brothers, where you were indoctrinated with the notion that it was your place to be helpful, put others first, and not have any opinions – because you were a girl. God rest my father's soul – he was a highly intelligent man, but he was hugely threatened until his death at 91, by the fact that he and I were so alike. It would have been far more nurturing for him to embrace and celebrate the similarities, rather than diminish me, but he was a product of his upbringing – as we all are. This brings me to the point of stating, loud and clear, about the liberating freedom of FREE CHOICE.

I'm here to tell you that there's no sell–by date in exercising that power. Free choice is about doing what you want, when you want, with whom you want. Like the legendary bluebird of happiness, I've found that while you've got breath in your body – it's never too late to override your poisonous inner story and end up with a happy script!

Exterminate! Exterminate!

If you're of a similar vintage to me, you'll recall the original appearance of the Daleks in Doctor Who. First appearing in 1963, they would go around (but not up stairs) destroying everything in their path whilst declaring "Exterminate! Exterminate!" I want you to learn to *exterminate* that faulty inner voice which threatens to sabotage your chances of finding love and your happiness when it rears its ugly head. For example, when your faulty inner voice tells you that you daren't approach a guy you fancy, because you know he'll never fancy you, and that you'll surely get rejected – that's the time to exterminate it. Or, ditto, when you want to try out a new look, but The Voice informs you that you look hideous.

The ego is frankly just a monster pretending to be you. It's a nasty piece of work, a false, empty shell and isn't who you really are. If you listen to it droning on and take what it vomits at you to heart, then you may end up lonely, in the gutter.

Spot the self-sabotage

I'd like you to identify, then write down in your journal, the ways in which the saboteur harms you in all areas of your life. If you can't identify these, then it's time to ask for input again from your trusted buddy. Be very careful if your bestie is a woman, because women can be incredibly catty and some might actually derive satisfaction from seeing you fail, so choose wisely. You want somebody who's upbeat and whom you instinctively know has your best interests at heart, with no axes to grind, or sharp edges.

During my time at The International Dating Academy, self-sabotage I have seen (time and time again) has included:

- Triggering your APB – Automatic Praise Blocker. So, when somebody pays you a compliment, you dismiss it faster than water runs off a duck's back. For example, your outfit is praised and you respond with "oh that old thing? I've had it for ages" – or "oh it only cost me £2.50 in a charity shop".

- Wanting to fit in – you act "less than" who you really are because of your fear of not fitting in, or not wanting to be seen as too successful, for fear of making others jealous.
- Diminishing your achievements and attributes because you don't want to appear vain or big-headed.
- Giving in to bullying, or acquiescing to others' wishes, because you've got a bad case of FOMO – Fear of Missing Out.
- Being afraid to express your opinions because they differ from that of others.
- Dumbing down your qualifications, your social status, or where you live because you're scared it will make you unpopular.
- Staying with the same group of friends because the prospect of change feels far too challenging for you to go for it. You stay stuck because there's comfort in the familiar even though it actually sucks.
- You're so damned angry about your past that you take it out on everybody you meet. If this is the case, remember this – the word D-ANGER is just one letter away from ANGER. You may need to seek professional help or sign up for an anger management class.
- You're simply too petrified to put your heart on the line – either because you've been badly hurt or you're inexperienced. If it's causing you to sabotage all your opportunities, then you do need to get help. Perhaps you ought to look for a good therapist, who can hold your hand, whilst you process this sort of unhelpful psychological baggage.
- Whenever somebody tries to offer you constructive criticism, you feign interest, and then immediately respond with, "yes, BUT". The unspoken message here is that everything the well-meaning person just tried to say to you – is a load of bollocks. Your "but" cancels it out.

In your journal, under each line, leave a space. When you feel your list is complete, go back and under each sentence, write how you could have responded differently or modified your behaviour in order to get a positive outcome. Looking at the above, a modified behaviour would have been to *accept the compliment* for the first example, or to listen to the feedback and consciously avoiding pushing back.

The object of this particular exercise is to cast light onto faulty behaviour patterns which are impeding your happiness. Self-analysis leads to self-awareness, which results in personal growth and the opportunity for positive change. You transport yourself from victimhood into liberty. Labouring too much to unearth *where* self-sabotage comes from, or *who* did it to you, is of limited value. What you must focus on is taking action NOW with the knowledge you've unearthed.

Isla, a 53-year-old classical singer, was a chronic self-saboteur. Sometimes you literally have to pull yourself up sharply to cut yourself short in your tracks. I told Isla to put an inconspicuous rubber band on her left wrist, and every time she realised she was saying something derogatory about herself, she was to "ping" the band. In this way, she eventually became able to break a really bad habit.

Getting out of your head

Being of service to others is a fantastic way of getting out of your head, in a non-mind-altering way. When you do something to help another, you remove the focus from yourself. You stop navel gazing and your perspective changes because suddenly you realise that your lot isn't that bad after all.

In addition, the unexpected, but welcome payback is that you often receive more than you ever anticipated. You may not feel like doing it, but once you get off your butt, by undertaking estimable actions, then your whole perspective transforms.

Payback often takes the simple form of others' gratitude, and I believe in the transformative power of gratitude – to the point that I write a daily gratitude list in my journal. I suggest you do this too; find five things every day which you're grateful for. And there's always plenty to choose from – even if you initially ridicule this idea. In the darkest moments of adversity, you can prise a pearl out of the jaws of adversity.

If you think being of service can help shift your perspective (and it really can!), I suggest you volunteer for a local organisation. Don't use work or busyness as an excuse. There's always time to help another. Try it and you'll soon see that there's no downside, only benefit for yourself and the people you're helping. Plus – it gives you another interesting topic to talk about when you're looking for a partner.

As you can see, in the final analysis, overcoming your internal saboteur isn't just about positive thinking but about engaging in *positive living*. Stop the catastrophic thinking. If you insist on still being a projectionist, then apply for a job at your local cinema! Otherwise – ditch this bad habit. Why can't you have all the great things life has to offer? Have the courage of your new convictions. Swop your previous F.E.A.R. (Fuck Everything and Run) mentality – and in its place, substitute your new, courageous convictions.

Flo, a 36-year-old biochemist, had been suffering from what I can only describe as near terminal self-obsession. This didn't exactly make her the ideal companion for her good pals, never mind a new man. Her incessant whingeing put everybody off. However, after volunteering at a children's hospice once a week, she soon realised that there were many people who were far worse off than her. Pretty soon the whingeing stopped and she was able to focus outwards, rather than inwardly.

WOEs → WOWs (Words of Wisdom)

♥ You never have to justify your actions – you deserve to be seen and heard!

♥ Having a victim mentality will never serve you in any way – ditch it.

♥ Being of service to others counteracts unhelpful self-obsession.

♥ Be compassionate with yourself.

♥ The former edicts regarding women no longer apply.

♥ There's no sell-by date on happiness.

PART 3

MOVING FROM FIRST DATE

TO SOULMATE

CHAPTER 11

THE FIRST THREE DATES – EMBRYONIC DATING

When is a relationship a relationship?

This chapter is all about the issues that can arise during early dating. Like early pregnancy, you have to take extra special care because your choices and actions during this period can have significant ramifications.

There is no blueprint for what to do because we're all individuals. I can merely advise you that you need to go by your instincts.

In turn, there's no downside to taking things very slowly, practising mindful reflection, before you make what are potentially very big moves. Never has any harm been done by practising mindful reflection!

The Great Unveiling (Sex)

I'm putting sex at the top of the list of issues to consider when you are embarking on a new relationship. And that's because it's potentially such a loaded, thorny issue. It's a tricky one to analyse because different people have varying needs and experiences, and there are more ways of getting this crucial component of any relationship wrong than right. Don't go round asking everyone for their opinion as to when you should have sex. Opinions are like backsides – everyone has one, but each is individual!

But, before you intertwine bodies and lock genitals, I urge you to ask yourself if you really do actually *like* this guy. If you don't like him, then quit while you're still ahead. If you do like him, then go for it, but only when you're ready.

Becky, a 44-year-old business owner, was extremely keen on Ralph, a 48-year-old civil engineer. Ralph had just come out of a traumatic relationship and just wasn't interested, initially, in having a sexual relationship with Becky. This, though, went completely against Becky's grain, as she felt super confident about her past performance as a seductress. The trouble was that although she'd had multiple sexual partners, none of them had ever really amounted to much more than a one night stand. She definitely wanted more from Ralph, whom she realised she actually liked. It was tough for her to reverse such an ingrained pattern, but with lots of mindful breathing and pausing, Becky went at Ralph's pace, and their relationship remained asexual for many months. When IT finally happen, Becky said the wait was worth it!

Try being friends first and foremost

Sex – such a small word which can cause so much angst for both men and women. Women worry about looking like a slut and desperate, and men (believe it or not) may face performance anxiety with a new partner. Let's face it – YOU can fake it, but he can't! Not that I'm advocating pretending to be in the throes of The Big O, if the nearest you've been to feeling the earth move today is a hearty sneeze.

Not only are we subjected to a barrage of "should" and "should nots" from the media, superimposed on that is our upbringing, education and previous sexual experiences – or lack of them – which can make or break a woman's libido. Add to that, some women have a dread of exposing their ageing bodies to a new partner, whilst probably also comparing themselves to some nubile and lithe young thing from his past (should he be dumb enough to open his great big gob too early on in the budding relationship). Don't you be bragging either – it's a recipe for disaster. This isn't the time to blab about your past lovers, nor convey the notion that the only thing that hasn't been over you is a bus!

I also believe there's a whole load of bollocks spoken about women and sex. It's my experience that sex is an instinctive urge for men, but for women it's generally got to be part of a committed relationship for it to be most enjoyable and fulfilling. Ultimately, good sex starts with good communication. There will be much more on learning the art of excellent communication in subsequent chapters. If you like the guy as a friend first, then the chances of everything else working out are far greater than if you jump in the sack at the first opportunity.

Here are some points to consider *before* having sex – and some pertinent reasons for *not* having sex:

- **Practising safe sex**. Okay, this may not be the most romantic of conversations, but you have to have it early on – before you have sex, in relation to any nasties you might catch, or an unwanted pregnancy. In this day and age, you can't brush sexually transmitted diseases under the carpet. Any responsible man won't be offended and if he is – then it's time to exit before it gets hot and heavy. You must value yourself and your body.
- **Giving in to pressure to have sex**. You should never be pressured into having sex. Ever. Using your body in order to get love or approval *never* works. We've all done it at some point, only to be badly disappointed and possibly left feeling cheap and nasty in the process. You also don't have

to engage in kinky sex unless it floats your boat, and you never have to engage in any sexual practice which is abhorrent to you.

- **Doing IT because everyone else is**. Comparisons are contemptuous! What everyone else is or isn't doing is none of your business, and unless you're psychic, you don't know anyway. All that matters is how YOU feel and when you're ready to take that major step.

Danger signs – when is a date a dud?

When you embark on a spanking new relationship, it's easy to wear rose-coloured glasses and dismiss anything that might get in the way of the initial, illusory state you find yourself in. I use the word illusory because when you're falling in luuuurve, all your hormones are going nuts, and can blast good old fashioned common sense, straight out of the window. Yes – it's important to relish the pink cloud stage of a relationship because, trust me, that phase doesn't last (which is just as well, or you'd never be able to concentrate on anything else for the rest of your life). The preoccupation associated with early lust gives way to a much more sustaining and endurable way of co-existing – if you play your cards right, and take heed of the warning signs.

Kimberly was a separated 40-year-old postgraduate research student. She was flattered when Jake, a 21-year-old undergraduate invited her out to a formal dinner at his university college. She did have misgivings, but her friends egged her on, assuring her it would be good for her ego, pulling her leg about being a cougar with a toy boy. Kimberly met Jake at a local pub, where he plied her with alcohol. More alcohol followed over dinner, and Kimberly felt a sense of impending doom, but ignored her instincts, and even joined Jake in smoking a few joints. Jake invited her back to his room for a supposed night cap. The minute the door slammed shut behind her, Jake said, "So, are we gonna have a shag, or what?" Instead of bolting, a stoned and sozzled Kimberly didn't reply, so Jake took this as her tacit consent. He then informed her he was going off on his bicycle to get some eco-friendly green condoms from the porter's lodge and that she should "slip into something more comfortable" in his absence. Thankfully, Kimberly began to sober up in Jake's absence, and departed hastily before his return. She had a lucky escape, but this demonstrates how you should always listen to your instincts – before you get into hot water.

Spotting a no-hoper

The following scenarios are amongst the ones which should automatically trigger your bright red no-hoper alert, and cause you to bail out of the relationship without further ado. My list isn't exhaustive but gives you indications of what to spot – and avoid.

Liar, liar – pants on fire

When you find out somebody's lying to you, it's an appalling basis for any relationship. Everybody tells white lies, but I'm referring to great big, fat porkies. If something your guy tells you just isn't stacking up – you don't need to know the chapter and verse of why – you just need to get the hell out of there. Whether it be about money, a job, kids, an ex-partner – it's a really bad sign. If you don't exit now, it's only going to be more painful and more humiliating further downstream. You should never be desperate and put up with any form of lying or deception.

Changing plans at the last minute

When you've agreed to do something together, and he lets you down at the last minute without a valid reason – this is a red flag. A valid reason being, for example, his kid who's living with him is ill, his mother died, his dog has to be put down, or there's a work crisis. They are all kosher reasons. I can't tell you precisely what's an invalid reason, because I'm not you. However, if you smell a rat – that's probably because you're dating one. Time to say "ciao bello".

The stringer

He strings you along, promising you the moon. He tells you how important you are to him, and what an incredible future you have together. He's romantic and, on the face of it, ticks all the boxes – but somehow, you instinctively feel that the relationship just isn't moving forward. His promises are empty and you start to realise that he's actually reciting his piece from a well-practised script.

Violence

An absolute non-starter and time to eject faster than 007 from the seat of his Aston Martin. Violence in any form towards you and yours is totally unacceptable. Some forms of violence, apart from the obvious physical thumping of you, include belittling you either in public or private, all forms of humiliation, emotional blackmail, and bullying. Messing with your head is just as bad as pushing you around. You deserve so much better. Walk. Immediately. The same goes for a jealous man who spies on you, doesn't allow you to go out with your friends, or interrogates you Gestapo-style every time you see him. This is controlling, intolerable behaviour.

Stephanie, a 39-year-old PR manager, was newly involved in a tempestuous relationship with Adam, a 40-year-old bookmaker. Adam suffered from pathological jealousy and was extremely controlling. The final straw came for Stephanie when one night, while she was out with a group of girlfriends at the cinema, Adam poured the entire contents of a pot of bright red paint through her letter box.

Money

If he makes you pay for everything or asks to borrow money, this is a no no. In embryonic dating, it's fair to take turns paying. Or at least to offer to pay and if he insists on paying for you then graciously accept. But when you go out, if it's expected that you're going to cough up every time, then take it as a warning. Ditto if he asks to borrow money, or asks you to pay off his debts. How many women have been taken in by this kind of behaviour, only to feel totally and utterly stupid a while later? Start as you mean to go on, right from the outset and take turns.

Addictions

This is a tricky one and an individual decision. I'd be a hypocrite if I advised you to avoid anyone with a history of addiction because I'm a recovering addict myself (with 20 years of continuous alcohol sobriety). I also suffered from musical addictions for the worst part of my life meaning that if I wasn't battling one damn addiction, I was having to confront another. BUT – and it's a huge BUT – there's an enormous difference between being a recovering addict, who's taking ongoing responsibility for acknowledging they have a permanent disease (and desisting from "using" in any shape, fashion or form), and a practising addict, who shows absolutely no sign of facing up to their demons, and getting help. If it's the latter, then there's nothing you can do to save this person. Only they can do so, and you're frankly better off out of it. I may sound harsh, but I speak from my own experience and that of other recovering addicts. Addiction isn't a moral issue, and nobody wakes up one day and decides they want to be an addict, but there IS a responsibility not to act out on this addiction. And addictions can be multiple and complex – including alcohol, sex, porn, gambling, spending, overeating, drugs, and workaholism, to name but a few.

You know, or suspect, he's still dating

You've agreed to stop seeing other people (which I don't advise before date three), and you've spotted that his online profile is still 'up', or again something he says or does, isn't stacking up. Or – even worse – you catch a dose of a Sexually Transmitted Disease. If you're unfortunate enough to catch an STD, you're going to have to confront him, because this is so risky to your own health and that of others. Please don't believe his protestations that you must have caught it from an infected toilet seat. You well know that you can't catch it from that, any more than you can get pregnant from a toilet seat. As tempting as it may be to allow his philandering willy to go gangrenous green, you've got to tell him! Please see below, my caveat about giving up seeing others too soon.

Dating a separated man

This is another toughie. How do you know for sure that his previous relationship is truly over and that there's no chance of reconciliation, which could mean major disappointment for you? A rough rule of thumb might be this: if he's still living with his partner, pending separation, leave well alone and remain friends, until he's moved out and you see definite evidence that he's free to date. If he balks at this suggestion, then it's fishy, and you're better off without him. Of course, there are always exceptions to every rule, but sticking to the 'friends thing' will never get you into hot water, whereas jumping in feet first without any caution, may well do. And never, EVER, date a man who's still married! They rarely leave their wives so don't be fooled! If you ignore this advice, you'll end up drowning in a great big can of worms for sure.

Marina, a 46-year-old legal executive, had started dating Jeff, a 48-year-old academic. Everything seemed to be hunky dory, until Jeff started to call her up in the wee small hours, talking dirty to her and ordering Marina to pretend that she was having sex with her dog. As if that wasn't bad enough, Jeff would only ever see Marina or speak to her, when it suited him. He was cagey about where he lived and was incredibly evasive about what he did outside working hours. One night, Marina asked her best friend Bunty to follow Jeff home from work. Bunty obliged and it turned out that Jeff was married with three kids.

Periods of adjustment

Now is the time to start to develop the art of good communication and to establish some rudimentary boundaries. Again, there will be more on boundaries, anon. These can include establishing how often you see each other, and how you communicate between dates. You can also explore which interests you share and those in which you differ. You don't have to do everything together and it's actually very healthy to maintain separate interests throughout a long term relationship. If you start moaning about the amount of time he plays golf or goes sailing with his mates, I guarantee, that at this early stage, such behaviour will be terminal. If you manage your expectations of each other now, you're less likely to run into trouble later on. Also, try as much as possible to establish you have the same priorities in life, e.g. regarding sex, religion, and politics – and identify which are deal-breakers for you. If you're a Marxist and he's a Conservative – never the twain shall meet.

The multi-pronged approach

Unless you've agreed not to date other people, don't even think about giving up your other options until after the first three dates, and assume he's doing the same too. Treat this statement as a relationship public health warning! Engaging in the multipronged approach will help to keep things light. It has to be a case of "slowly,

slowly catchy monkey". I've been out with, and married, a couple of apes myself, so I tell you this from heartfelt experience. Rome wasn't built in a day and neither is an enduring relationship. As the Arab proverb says, "Trust in Allah – but tether your camel."

WOEs → WOWs (Words of Wisdom)

♥ To thine own self, be true – always remember you're your number one priority.

♥ If in doubt – get out.

♥ Discuss and agree on your dating and inter-date etiquette.

♥ Continue managing your expectations as the relationship develops.

♥ Inconsistency in a partner is a warning sign – discover, uncover and discard what doesn't serve you.

♥ Don't take yourself or what happens too seriously – give time… time.

CHAPTER 12

BECOME A SUCCESSFUL BAGGAGE HANDLER

The blended family

"And they ALL lived happily ever after", as the *fairy tale* goes. Did they, hell. Note the italics, because when you're a stepparent, even in the very best of cases – which are few and far between – it's a near impossible job. If you think being a natural parent is tough, then try out step parenting for size. According to the US Step Family Foundation, 13,000 new step families form every day. It's predicted that, soon, the blended family will become more the norm than the traditional family, whose associated mores have all but broken down. That affords the opportunity for a great deal of complexities.

Ok, so we all have baggage. But when you take on a partner, it's a case of *"love me, love my dog"*, and some dogs are just plain nasty, and bite viciously, no matter how many delicious bones you offer them. Some of that baggage is weightier than others. When you enter a new relationship, you bring all your past emotional history, good and not so good.

Stepping up to the plate – the truth, the whole truth, and nothing but the truth

No matter how *bad* the birth parent was (or is), and even if mummykins is devoid of a single maternal cell and would flog her kids on eBay given half a chance, as a stepparent you have no voice, nor any rights – legal and otherwise, in the raising of the child. There's no exterior body of support, as there is for single parents, or even grandparents these days. And with the best will in the world – your partner may go through the murky motions of seeking your opinions, but will probably discard them, feeling caught between a rock and a hard place. The word "injustice" takes on a whole new meaning when you become a step.

Let the games begin

Step parenting is actually an unnatural state. As someone who's had 15 years' experience of being a stepparent, and married a man who has heavy duty baggage, I can tell you that there's no easy answer to the inner conflicts and the moral dilemmas, which being a stepparent will stir up. The best thing you can do to preserve your relationship – and your sanity – is to distance yourself, behind a self-protective emotional Berlin Wall… and keep your mouth shut. You can try until you're blue in the face, but in the vast majority of cases, your input won't be appreciated and may well be thrown back in your face. You run the risk of casting yourself in the ongoing role of emotional punch bag, and scapegoat, and be the recipient of prolific unconscious projection, spewed all over you, from all sides. The issues may actually have nothing to do with you, but boy are you going to end up being the target. Like it or not, you're public enemy number one.

Stepparent survival kit

There comes a point when you have to decide what's important – the health of your relationship with your nearest and dearest or the time-limited surge of power which comes from being *right* about The Baggage. For example, you find an empty bottle of alcohol stashed under your teenage step kid's bed, after a visit, and you suspect they have an issue with booze. You try and convince your partner of this, but he remains in denial. You can either keep banging on about it – or let events unfold, as they surely will, if your suspicions are correct. Isn't better to be happy (sort of) than right? If not, you risk stirring up an avalanche of raw emotion and end up driving yourself and your partner into that crazy-making, hideously familiar emotional cul de sac. Then you beat your head against the wall and repeat this all over again, illustrating once more, Einstein's theory perfectly – that madness is doing the same thing over and over again, expecting different results.

Sisterhood "therapy" – your kvetching network

Given the lack of external support, I firmly believe in the therapeutic powers of The Sisterhood. Regular rendezvous where you can safely vent your spleen, dissipating The Daily Frustration of *guess what they did THIS time*?

The bottom line is – if you're brutally honest – your step children don't want you, now or ever, and frankly you don't need the hassle and upset of having to cope with them. They were in search of their own happy ever after, exclusive of you – two birth parents under the same roof. Harsh but, alas, true.

Your kvetching network is a trusted group of close-mouthed women, in similar situations, whom you see regularly, and with whom you can safely let rip. Often you'll discover that an injustice shared, is an injustice halved. And you don't have to even meet to do this. SOS texting, phone calls, or email can work just as well. You're ploughing a solitary furrow, which can feel like a very long and lonely road, so avail yourself of as much support as you can. It's not negative thinking to do this – it's sanity- and relationship-preserving, because it acts as a safety valve for your pent-up emotion. THIS is the place to quip that his ex was so unattractive that she must have tricked him into marrying him, by dint of a shotgun wedding. Don't ever say that to him or you'll portray yourself in a very unfavourable light!

Beware of do-gooders

These are the supposed well-meaning friends, family or professionals who tell you that you have to always remember that you're the adult and the step kid is the child (no matter how old they may be); tacit code for you to 'like it or lump it'. These are also mostly people who've never had to endure the difficulties of step family enmeshment. This is why I urge you to forge your own support network, so you can give these silly people a major "body swerve", as we say in Glasgow.

Unrealistic expectations – yours and his

It's really difficult for both of you. He'd love you to become a surrogate mother to his kids at one level, if their own mother was crap, but on the other hand (depending on your personal circumstances) this may prove absolutely impossible due to toxic family dynamics. You can whinge about it all you want, but the fact is that you have to work with what actually is, rather than what he or you would like it to be. You're powerless to change him, but you do have full control over your own reactions. This is a situation which demands constant, ongoing effort, as well as clarity of communication, demonstrating great sensitivity to the way in which the other person feels. There's just no point going in there with guns blazing, as you'll only risk damaging your relationship, which absolutely has to remain your top priority. Both of you have to be open and flexible to compromise, no matter how toxic the familial backdrop may prove to be.

Ex-wives, ex-lives, and additional complications

Given that blended families can all be problematic, there are some situations which prove über toxic, and over and above the call of your duty. There are those ex-wives and ex-partners who can't or won't move on, for whatever reason. Here are but a few examples of potential relationship-wreckers, which you may encounter:

Litigation

This is one of the most destabilising experiences you can go through, and it can drag on for years, thanks to malicious exes and our cumbersome (and often incompetent) legal system. No matter how amicable the split may have been, very often, if a new partner appears on the scene – whether or not you're responsible for the split, history gets rewritten, and a dog fight may break out over money or step kids, even just as a decoy. As somebody whose husband was dragged through the courts and crucified by a man-hating, woman judge, I can vouch for just how dramatic an effect that can have on your relationship.

Other stepmothers, like myself, have had to take out injunctions against number one. Your own financial affairs which have absolutely nothing to do with your partner's arrangements with his ex, will get hauled into vogue and scrutinised. Boundaries are violated and the whole experience is nothing short of traumatic.

Many an ex has unscrupulously used kids as pawns to extricate more cash from your man, and also to manipulate him emotionally. She may even have transformed into a latter day version of The Bunny Boiler, as in the film "Fatal Attraction", and all the while you're expected to somehow take it on the chin, smiling sweetly, as you do a Tammy Wynette and Stand by Your Man. Yeah, right!

You can end up having such horrendous arguments, including crashing, throwing stuff around and exploding with justified frustration, that your home ends up resembling the aftermath of a teenager's party. It can all get super ugly – including your and his behaviours.

Francesca had the horrendous experience of discovering that her husband's ex had, unbeknownst to either herself or her husband, paid a visit to their holiday home in Spain, where her teenage twin step-daughters, were staying. The ex and the step-daughters had thrown a wild party, had gotten completely stoned out of their heads on cannabis, and had thought it extremely amusing to deposit bricks down the toilets, thereby causing £800 worth of damaged drains.

A bad dose of the green-eyed monster

There's nothing more dangerous than an ex scorned. She may be hell bent on destroying your relationship, and will stop at nothing to achieve her resentful aims. Unfortunately, this is all too common an occurrence, and it's largely based on her irrational jealousy. For example, if the ex hasn't found somebody else, you can expect a whole crock of shit to come your way, and you better start praying that she does find somebody PDQ. Exes like this are vile. They failed to achieve happiness with your man, they're stuck in victim mode big time, and they get off on the buzz of causing you endless hassle. Their self-pitying agenda is so overwhelmingly horrendous, that you're damned if you do – and damned if you don't try to make the peace with them.

The disturbances can manifest themselves in a number of intrusive ways. Phone calls at all hours, announcing so-called emergencies, resulting in your experiencing unwelcome coitus interruptus. Demands to go round and do a free bit of odd jobbing at the drop of a hat. Visits to police stations. Extortionate legal bills. Frustrating meetings with social services. Dumping the kids on you when she knows damn well that you're about to go out to celebrate something meaningful, or going on holiday. Poisoning the kids and setting them up to ask you a number of highly personal questions about your circumstances, which are none of their damned business, such as how often you have sex – or who pays for what in your household. Some of us have even received hate mail and voodoo dolls. The list and toxic variations thereon is, frankly, inexhaustible.

Troubled step kids

Again, these come in all formats. Typically, girls will have it in for you far more than boys, because of inherent female competition for their first love, their daddy factor. You often have to develop a big heart and a short memory. That's very easy to say, but in practical terms is incredibly hard to achieve. Whether you've "inherited" serene little darlings or the Hitler Yoof, who are hiding out in the former matrimonial bunker just waiting to launch the next hand grenade at you, the fact is that they are his kids, and if you put him in too impossible a situation you may well end up being booted out on your arse, and back to square one again – alone. In order to stay in the relationship for the long haul, you have to carry on doing some stringent work on yourself from the moment you enter that relationship, until kingdom come. This means forcibly reminding yourself of all of the positive reasons you're with this man, what you mean to each other, and to focus on these great aspects, rather than on the problematic step kids. Often you just have to settle for a state of détente, in the absence of anything better. If you can't stand the heat of this essential ongoing inner work, then I suggest you get out of the kitchen now, before you embroil yourself further. If you don't get (and keep) a firm grip on yourself, you'll blow the relationship.

Yours, mine and ours

Another factor which can come into play for you is sadness that you don't have any kids with the love of your life, and you're not going to have any. Either it's too late – you're hitting or have gone through the menopause – or he just refuses point blank to have any for his own reasons. This can feel like an ongoing, festering wound at the core of your relationship, especially if you have troublesome step kids, and even more so if you've never had a child of your own, or have lost a much-loved child.

You do yourself a major disservice if you allow yourself to muse for too long, on what might have been, if only he'd relented, or you'd met sooner. You're going to have to thrash this one out between you. As for all of the other tricky issues, you may well benefit for seeking professional help (about which I'll write more later on).

The same caveat applies for when you introduce each other to your various kids. You have to wait until you really truly are an item, and that may take months. Otherwise, you can get into an almighty mess, for absolutely no reason at all. It's better to wait a bit too long, than to make the introductions too soon after a previous relationship break up, when emotions are running high and feelings are raw. And while I'm at it, you don't have to take any crap from his extended family, any more than he should have to take any from yours. You have to discuss this calmly with him, tell him how you feel and then make a decision as to how to proceed in the future. Either you still see them, and remember the bigger picture – your relationship – or, if you find their company too offensive, then distance yourself, and allow him to see them without you being present.

Boundaries and compartmentalisation

Boundaries are about setting mutually acceptable limits. Compartmentalisation relates to having complete separation of time and certain parts of your lives. You can have both or one without the other, dependent upon how you feel about the baggage. Remember you're human and so is he. You're going to screw up again and again, and if there's love, you'll have to learn to keep forgiving each other – and yourselves. It's vital that you forge a way forward and agree some boundaries. You may be able to do this yourselves, but if not, once again, it's important to seek professional help. I've repeatedly made loads of mistakes so I'm definitely not preaching from a place of step parenting perfection!

Try to agree difficult issues in bite-sized chunks. Hot topics are what to do on holidays, family functions, and how to spend joint money on your kids and step kids.

Also, you need to discuss and make time for boundaried intimacy which can't be shattered, except under the most extreme emergency – and only by mutual agreement. If you know you've got to bring up a hot topic, then perhaps go out and do it in a public place, where you won't lose it, and don't raise tough stuff either late at night or first thing in the morning, as it's got the potential to wreck your sleep or bugger up your day.

In the final analysis, successful step parenting is also about behaving mindfully and cooling your hot impulse. These complex issues will bring out your worst psychological wounding and your feelings of childlike injustice. Mindfulness is a powerful antidote in moments of extreme distress.

Pippa and her partner, Justin, went on holiday together, for the first time, with his 13-year-old son Calum. Calum made his loathing of his potential new stepmother, extremely clear. Every morning, when she stepped into the shower, Pippa was greeted by a great big turd. Dutifully she said nothing, and cleared it up. The right thing would have been to tell Justin about this, immediately, rather than to allow the seething inner rage to build up, which resulted in a major explosion several months later – a near relationship combuster. Nobody in their right mind should have tolerated this kind of behaviour and, if Justin didn't back her up there and then, at the time of the grotesque incident, then her boundaried response to this should have been to leave the relationship.

Step kids verboten

The following are completely off limits when dealing with step kids:

- Don't criticise or discipline them. If you've got anything to say, try to do so calmly to your partner, when the step child is out of earshot.
- If your step child is horrid to their father, you're powerless to do anything about it. Focus on looking after yourself, instead of letting rip at him about how awful they are. He probably knows this anyway, at some level, but hates to admit it to himself, never mind you!
- *Never* compare his kids to yours.
- Don't criticise their mother to them. It'll only end in tears – yours.
- Don't bad mouth any of your step kids' extended family.
- Remember that you're not their mother. The best you can aspire to, is to eventually become a friend; expecting more will just lead to disappointment, involving putting your head on the chopper only to be hurt again.
- Your task is first and foremost self-care and preservation of your hard won relationship.

And it's fucking difficult.

Tools and other self-help

Years ago, I attended a weekend anger management course, in an attempt to help me deal with the challenges of my own particular step family situation. However, I couldn't take it seriously, after witnessing, on the very first day, one of the trainers bashing a pile of cushions with a cricket bat, yelling, "Drink your juice, you little shits"! That doesn't mean, however, that there aren't some kosher anger management courses around. There are plenty of organisations who provide them. You just have to search online and ask for recommendations, so you avoid the dodgy ones.

Perhaps you need to go and scream obscenities in the shower, or bash your pillow whilst visualising Mama Hitler's face, go for a run and yell in the forest, or carry out some ritualistic cutting of any associated, and now unwanted, memorabilia belonging to your partner and his ex. Do tread with caution though. As much as it serves YOUR need for release, and gives you immense satisfaction, watching his buggered up past being shredded by the recycling machine at your local Tesco's, he may not appreciate it!

Perhaps write a letter to the ex and steps, telling them how badly treated you feel, or how totally unacceptable their behaviour is. However – *you do not send this letter* – because if you do, I can guarantee that all hell will break loose! Also, don't leave it lying around anywhere, lest your partner finds it and reads it. This tool is especially helpful when you feel badly wronged and you feel that you've got no voice, or your voice has been dumbed right down or even cut right out – by a load of "shoulds" and "musts", inflicted on you by your beloved and others.

I believe strongly in the power of gratitude. So, here's an exercise in reframing. Instead of moaning about how hard done by you are, write down three things which are brilliant about your situation, and for which you're grateful. There must be three things or you wouldn't have stayed in the relationship this far. I realise this is tough, but if you think about it, you can choose to use these awful situations to your benefit. These ghastly people actually make you stronger as a person. In that respect, pain can be your greatest teacher. It'll take you a while to get your head around this, but if and when you can succeed in doing this, you'll experience the whole scenario differently and notice that it's actually built up your moral fibre.

Mindfulness meditation is the tool which continues to help me the most, on a daily basis. When you practise mindfulness not just for 10 minutes, in one sitting, but engage in mindful moments throughout your day, you'll start to see the benefits. At first, the positive results are subtle, but over a period of time, you'll experience a quantum shift in your attitudes and will choose not to allow these silly people to wind you up! You'll no longer subject yourself to a daily shower of cortisol – the stress hormone which kicks off when you go into one – and you'll also relish your partner's undying gratitude, for not giving him ongoing earache, when he's stuck in an already ghastly situation. Better still – encourage your partner to also learn to meditate and then you can start the day together with a short period of meditation. We do that every morning at 7.15 am, and it's transforming our lives! We're both incredibly busy people and, as the saying goes, if you can't find the time to meditate for 20 minutes, then you need to meditate for an hour! Learn to breathe in the good shit and breathe out the bullshit. I promise – it really does help.

Getting professional help

As I've said before, asking for help is a sign of strength – a badge of courage. Sometimes you have to seek professional help for yourself/yourselves, in order to navigate stormy waters. Peter and I have availed ourselves of professional help at various periods in our relationship, jointly and separately. At one time we even attempted family therapy with his ex-wife and kids.

Perhaps your man is unconsciously throttled by guilt and you feel that because of this, he enables bad behaviour in his kids. The guilt can be about anything – e.g. leaving them with an appalling ex, not fighting harder for them, giving up on his marriage – or pretty much any other reason. There's never a shortage of things we can beat ourselves up about and, of course, given that we can't turn the clock back, it's a really good idea to seek help if we're emotionally stuck. Everybody will benefit from this. If one party in the dynamic changes, then the whole shooting match changes.

But – another major caveat is essential here. Always keep the spotlight on yourself, because you're the only person you can change! You can encourage your partner to seek help – but he may or may not choose to do so right now. He might if the situation gets really bad – but if he refuses to do so now, there's precious little you can do about this. If this is the case, then I urge you to just keep practising self-care, which is always your priority, over and above him or anybody else – kids included.

You may benefit from attending a 12 step programme such as Codependents Anonymous, which will help you detach from the drama, and focus on your own well-being. I provide details of this and similar organisations in the resources section of this book.

Keep the spotlight on you; you're the only one you can change.

Anna is proof positive that not all step parenting is bad news. Sometimes achieving harmony is possible, but, more often than not, only with a lot of help. Anna "inherited" three young children, after their mother abandoned them. There was a great deal of hostility towards her as the kids accused her of trying to take their mother's place. Anna's love for her partner was immense, so they decided to embark on some very painful family therapy, with an experienced therapist. It was a tough process but, in time, the issues were resolved in as satisfactory a manner as they could be, given the complex family dynamic. Anna now has a good relationship with her step kids, and has the wisdom to allow them the space to mourn the loss of their unavailable mother, without trying to plug that hole.

Stepparent stress busters

Nobody said that being part of a blended family was going to be easy. Indeed, it's been one of the biggest challenges of my life – and I've had plenty of dark experiences, so I'm well-qualified to state this. I know it is possible to stay happy, despite any external onslaughts, because we continue to work on ourselves and our relationship. Let me offer you some step parenting troubleshooting tips:

- **Remind yourself of what really matters.** Does it truly matter what the baggage may have said or done? If you keep harping on about it, then you'll keep re-experiencing it. The word "resentment" literally means "to feel again". Why would you want to repeatedly re-inflict pain on yourself? In the grand scheme of things, who gives a damn?

- **Focusing and loving each other.** Focus on what you like about your partner, not on what you dislike. Remind yourself why you fell in love with him. Reflect on what it was like before you got together. Use the positives to draw on, like a well of emotional sustenance, during the tough times.

- **Enjoy the time you spend together.** Plan special treats for your partner. During that time, talk exclusively about good things in your life, not the negatives. Devise a special warning – this could be a word or a hand gesture – and if one of you inadvertently trips into the danger zone of talking about the baggage, use this mechanism to call a halt.

- **Giving each other space.** Despite the very best of intentions, at times you're going to hit a brick wall and argue. In order not to escalate this, give each other space for a bit. This could be by one of you going out for a walk, or a run, or a cycle ride. Perhaps you can pound up and down in your local pool. Or go and visit a friend, or take a walk around an art gallery, or a trip to the cinema. Solitary experiences are great for providing you with an opportunity to step back and reflect – and get things back into proportion again.

Crunch time

There may come a time when you can't keep your mouth shut, and you feel it's decision time about whether you stay in the relationship or you leave. Remember – everyone has baggage – if they haven't, then they've not lived or may have lived an extremely sheltered life. Be brutally honest and ask yourself – do you really want to start again? Sometimes the grass will appear greener on the other side because it's been fertilised by bullshit.

No matter how nice you are, no matter what you do for your step kids, you'll probably always be the wicked stepmother. So build a bridge over yourself and get over it – and get on with your life. Don't major on minor issues. They're his kids, not yours. You're together because you care immeasurably for one another. Don't allow them to have so much importance in either your life or your relationship. It's an ongoing struggle and process for most of us. But don't give in! That's probably what they wanted in the first place – and you just need to learn to be smarter and more resilient than them. A great relationship is worth working at and fighting for. Don't give up on a good thing. Think in terms of what you've got to work with, and the fact that victory is even sweeter when you overcome adversity.

WOEs → WOWs (Words of Wisdom)

♥ You came, you saw, but you'll never conquer – blood is thicker than water, so don't put him in an impossible position of having to choose between you or them.

♥ Step parents can't afford to fall prey to divadom – it's tough, but doable.

♥ Don't throw the baby out with the bath water – expectations of the baggage are resentments in construction, so best not to have any.

♥ Acceptance of what is, wisdom and flexibility, are the keys to comfortable step parenting.

♥ Pain is inevitable – suffering isn't, so don't buy into the drama.

♥ Detachment equals freedom – Emotional disturbance just isn't worth it – and neither are they!

CHAPTER 13

MINDFUL LOVING – 13 SECRETS FOR
LASTING HAPPINESS

We all love a happy ending, and this chapter is about how you can go about achieving this with your long term partner. As time goes by, you'll surely develop your own ideas and strategies, but for now, here are my suggested top 13.

1. Good, open, honest communication

Mindfulness is an especially invaluable tool in the area of couple communication, where it's so easy to hear what we *think* is being said, through our personal filters, and then to overreact to it – strongly. More often than not, this is down to not only poor communication – but also our deeply personal, historical "stuff". As Tennyson said, "I am part of all I have met".

Achieving and maintaining good communication is lifelong, ongoing work. This is where practising communication mindfulness can be so helpful. When you put it into operation, you become increasingly able to pause, "mind the gap", and clarify what's *actually* being said. When you do this, you're far less likely to get your relationship knickers in a twist.

In our earlier days, we used to joke about our dreadful modus of communication. Peter would say something completely innocuous, and my filter would pick it up in a totally injurious way. One day Peter made light of it and piped up, *"Spillman he say he love you – Namllips he say you're a piece of shit"*. If you're quick on the trigger, you'll immediately realise that *Namllips is Spillman* backwards. I'm sure you get the point! I'm relieved to say that these days, Namllips is pretty much dormant, and only occasionally emerges for a brief airing, before we take corrective communication action. A huge factor contributing to our vastly improved communication is that we meditate together every morning. We both find that our short joint ritual pays relationship dividends. Poor communication will rapidly become a mental weed, clogging up and perhaps even strangling your precious relationship.

2. A fulfilling and imaginative sex life

It's only natural that once the chemical highs of early sex wear off, things can feel more hum drum. This is a good thing as, if you were trying to live for the rest of your days in such a lust-intoxicated state, slobbering and obsessing, until you get the next leg over, you'd never work another day in your life. However, this doesn't give you carte blanche to hang up your suspenders, and spend the rest of your days sporting faded granny drawers. You have to continue to make the effort.

One of our Dinner Dates members, Enzo, once tried to justify his chronic infidelity with his ex-wife. He explained that *"fucking your wife is like shooting a dead rabbit"*! That poor woman. Clearly, Enzo has plenty of work to do on himself before I'd deem him "fit for purpose" to begin a new relationship.

I do believe, however, that there isn't a single person, man or woman, who won't be led into an affair, under the right (or wrong) circumstances. It's naïve to be fooled into a state of what I refer to as The Big C. Complacency. The ultimate relationship rotter. It's possible to enjoy a fulfilling sex life until death do you part. And I can assure you, if you don't put in the action, somebody else will – with your man! It's the law of the jungle and there are plenty of predatory women out there who'll pinch your guy, given half a chance. Don't provide the fertile ground for this, by allowing your man to feel undesired.

Make an effort, and if you don't feel like having sex and he does, then find some other tactile way of pleasing him. As the saying goes, why have beef burger when you have steak at home? Of course, all of the above should work both ways – and it's up to you to communicate this to him just as sensitively. And there will be sticking points, along the way.

A sexual relationship is a voyage of ongoing discovery and, similarly, will at times have various twists and turns, as it runs its lifelong course. The following list is far from exhaustive, but some of these thorny issues may rear their ugly heads, so are worth a mention.

Most women hate their guy ogling porn and most guys do it. If you make a big deal about it, he'll probably do it in secret. Women fear that they're being compared to the tantalising nudes, doing God-knows-what – but the bottom line is, if you'll pardon the pun, that men are visual creatures, they're different from us, and they enjoy doing it, in an emotionally detached way. So you either have to accept it and join in, or turn a blind eye to it. Some women actually do enjoy using porn and can make it a part of their sexual routine – with and without a partner being present.

I'm not condoning the person who develops a full-blown addiction to porn, cybersex and chat rooms. I'm just trying to be the voice of reason here. It should be seen as an adjunct, but not a substitute for sex. If it becomes an addiction, then help needs to be sought.

If you experience a temporary change or mismatch in libido, you either need to find the maturity to discuss your difficulties together or with a professional sex therapist. If there are erectile problems or vaginal dryness, then your GP should be your first port of call.

Another area of hysteria centres on the subject of masturbation, solitary and mutual – in and out of a long term relationship. The hysteria may derive from childhood, thanks to parental, schooling and religious attitudes, but the associated shame that surrounds it is nonsensical. If it were true that it's harmful and will in some way mark you, then the whole world would be entirely populated by blind hirsute people, roaming around like rampant werewolves. Masturbation is normal within a committed relationship, so get real and don't worry about it. Besides which, without it, nobody would be in touch with what turns them on.

Affairs and infidelity are corrosive and can only cause extreme hurt to all concerned. Nothing "just happens" – least of all an affair – we make it happen. The cheap thrill and the temporary buzz of an illicit liaison, just isn't worth it. If you feel tempted, then be brave, be bold and have the balls to tell your partner – *before* you act on your urges. Affairs mess big time with your head and cause major damage. Fantasies are one thing – everybody has them, but better to share these with your partner, in the deep comfort of your conjugal bed, than to destroy your relationship. Don't be a mug. And if one of you does have an affair, then you must seek help to regroup, and work through your feelings and see how you recover and move forward. And speaking of mugs, I once received the following email, after writing about various topics to do with singletons, in my online column.

Dear Cynth'

I've been suspicious of my husband, Simon, for weeks, so today I followed him.

He told me he was going to the gym, but, baffled, I watched him draw up outside a flat in South London, where the door was opened by a creature I can only describe as a much younger (and incredibly vulgar) version of me. I grew so incensed, that I marched straight up to the door, banging on it loudly. Vulgar Version of Me answered it, looking totally flummoxed. Insisting that I knew my husband was in there, I demanded to speak to him. She tried to stop me going in, but I pushed her out of the way, frantically ran into every room and opened every cupboard, seeking my adulterous "quarry". When I eventually wrenched open the door of the airing cupboard, there was Simon, crouching on the floor, stark bollock naked, apart from his Armani spectacles which were quivering on the end of his nose - attempting to hide amongst sheets, pillow cases and towels.

Simon, as cool as the proverbial cucumber, calmly and indignantly exclaimed, "It's not what it looks like. You're just imagining things. Please go home, have a nice cup of tea and everything will be okay."

He's cheated on me twice before. Do you think I should believe him?

I'm destroyed but I still love Simon. I'm fat and 50 and am afraid of spending the rest of my life on my own, especially now that our 2 kids have flown the nest. I felt I should ask you what to do as you've been married so many times, and are ballsy.

Yours,

Devastated

I don't suffer fools gladly – as you'll have worked out by now – and this was my response:

Wake up and smell the coffee. Simon seems to regard you as part of the furniture – do you really want to be conveniently used as somebody else's commode to dump on? In my humble opinion, if you choose to answer in the affirmative, then it's not just Simon who's simple.

Get a life. Your own.

I wish you well.

Cynth'

Need I say anything more?

3. Interdependency versus co-dependency

I really like Kahlil Gibran's poem on marriage in which he advises, "Let there be spaces in your togetherness". This doesn't mean either of you should abandon the other, but that it's healthy for you to spend time apart as well as together, which is vastly different from cloying togetherness. Your long term relationship is actually enhanced by separate activity and even absence – which definitely causes the lust to grow fonder. Co-dependency sucks the very life out of your relationship. Interdependency enhances it. Don't be afraid of it.

It's also essential that you keep your network of female friends and that you engage with them frequently. You mustn't allow yourself to become one of those women who drop their friends at a moment's notice, because your partner suddenly becomes free, when you're supposed to be going out with your pals.

4. Continued mental stimulation

I've seen this in action – or even inaction. People define their week by when the next episode of "EastEnders" is on and their conversation revolves around what's on the box. This is bad. There's a whole world out there just waiting to be discovered and rediscovered. There are courses to be taken, new interests to be pursued, people to be met. Expand your horizons for your own and your relationship's sake. I'm not berating watching TV, of course, but the point is if you want to maintain a dynamic, healthy relationship, then remain open to lifelong learning and new experiences. Keep expanding that grey matter and you'll never regret it.

5. Ongoing renegotiation about miscellaneous boundaries

Relationships don't remain static because they're a living entity with a life force of their very own. This is why you need to keep revising and renegotiating your boundaries, as time goes on. To give one classic example, it's vitally important that you discuss and decide upon what happens to your assets, joint and individual, before one of you shuffles off your mortal coil. If you don't, and there are children left behind, then you may leave them one hell of a mess to sort out. The most efficient way of avoiding blended family chaos is to draw up a will with a competent professional who's qualified to do so. A W.H. Smith DIY kit just won't do.

I heard of a client who, when on his death bed, was discovered never to have divorced his first wife, whilst bigamously "marrying" number two. What a calamity! And, once you have got an up to date will, you must review it regularly, so it reflects your current circumstances. People think it's morbid to discuss this but invariably, once it's done, a great sense of relief is universally felt. There's a joke in the will writing trade that goes, statistics demonstrate that you live eight years longer than your last will – so if you want to live forever, keep having a new will drafted!

6. Respecting differences and appreciating and expanding on the similarities

Accept the things you can't change about your partner and keep the spotlight on yourself – the only person you truly ever can change. And when you do change, then the whole dynamic of your relationship shifts. Keep the focus and your energy on fixing yourself. Anything else is a spurious waste of time and effort.

7. Being first and foremost friends

I'm assuming that you've heeded all my previous advice – and you really like this guy that you're embroiled with, for the long haul. He should be your best friend – not your only one – but the person who's clearly one hundred percent in your corner, come what may. Best friends do argue, of course, but ultimately the bond that binds them together overcomes all the difficulties that may threaten to separate them. Treat him like you'd treat any best friend: with love, patience, and compassion. Before you have something tricky to say, ask yourself if it really has to be said, does it have to be said now, and what's the kindest way of saying it – and breathe, before you say it.

8. Keeping romance alive

It's so important to keep romance alive. Sizzling-in-the-sauna sex starts outside of the bedroom. It's the little touches that count. Refuse to allow the trivia of life to eradicate romance from your lives. Make time for love. Have a "dirty weekend" at home. Leave notes for each other around the house. Call each other during the day just to say you miss each other. Email to say you're thinking about your partner.

Never reduce your kissing to a mere perfunctory peck on the cheek at the beginning and the end of the day. Cuddle up on the sofa and snog like you used to do in the early days. Sleep naked. Burn candles and incense. Ban social media from the bedroom – it should be a technology-free zone – so no mobiles. The world won't end because you're off social media for eight hours. Have baths together. Give each other a non-sexual massage with aromatherapy oils. Use your imaginations. Buy him a bouquet of his favourite flowers. Plan a surprise trip away for your partner. Read poetry aloud. When he travels on business, slip a love letter into his suitcase, unnoticed. I'm blessed with a super romantic husband who once invited me by formal invitation to a black tie dinner, cooked by himself, in our kitchen, which was ablaze with every candle we possess in the house. After dinner, we danced. It was dynamite! And if you can't think of anything original – then use google – the internet is full of brilliant ideas.

42-year-old Tanya, a luxury boutique owner, was married to Ryan, a very wealthy 45-year-old horse racer. Ryan felt that intimacy between them had gone out of the window and – given his glamorous profession and financial status (plus the fact that he was drop dead gorgeous) – there were always plenty of women making a play for him, Ryan managed the situation well, until he met Lauren, a 24-year-old blonde model, at one of his stables. He found himself strongly attracted to Lauren, and every time he saw her, it really messed with his head. Given the lack of intimacy at home, he felt he was close to doing something with Lauren, he might later regret. Ryan tried to discuss this with his best friend, Carl, a confirmed bachelor. Carl didn't appreciate either the seriousness of the situation, nor Ryan's trust in him and even made a joke out of it, quipping that the pull of one pubic hair was stronger than the pull of three wild horses – and that Ryan should just "go for it" because, in any case, Tanya would never know. But, much as he was tempted, Ryan decided to somehow find the guts to tell Tanya about his attraction to Lauren. Naturally, Tanya was deeply upset, but she did admire Ryan for having the honesty to 'fess up – and they became committed to improving their joint lives and especially their intimacy quotient. Tanya also realised that Ryan was also partly suffering from a male midlife crisis and was philosophical that lust does happen – but you don't have to act on those feelings of lust. This near-miss actually improved their relationship over time.

9. Being able to say sorry

Unlike the bollocks you may have seen in the film "Love Story" –love IS having to say you're sorry – even when strictly, you're not. The pain of discipline versus the pain that stems from the regret of not apologising is infinitely better. I'm not saying you should be a scapegoat and take the blame for everything. It's about achieving a happy medium, and focusing on what's good in the relationship – not the noise which you may spew in the heat of the angry moment.

Don't throw the baby out with the bath water by allowing your motor mouth to disengage from your heart and wise self. Words are painful weapons and can't be taken back once said. If you do end up arguing, because you're only human, then try to fight clean and know when to stop if it's in danger of getting ugly. Have a particular signal you both recognise, such as raising your index finger, which calls an immediate halt to matters; a signal that indicates you need to have some time out. Then park the discussion until things are calmer. And don't commit financial adultery by pissing away money, just to get back at him. Act your age, not your shoe size!

10. Showing continuing appreciation of, and gratitude for, the other.

There's magic in the ordinary, in gestures of tenderness especially under stress. Demonstrating thoughtfulness doesn't have to involve spending money or displays of ostentation. Write a gratitude list of each other's positive traits and attributes – essential when you're pissed off with each other as it will remind you of why you fell for one another. Go through pictures and mementos of your early days and also your special ones. Never forget anniversaries, birthdays and significant days. Show each other consideration. Express your appreciation to each other for what you CAN do. Don't forget how horrid it was being single!

11. Learning to grow through adversity

Shit happens to all of us and nobody is exempt from suffering. You may face unemployment, the empty nest syndrome when your kids leave home, illness or family bereavement, to name but a few possible scenarios. Continue to share your wishes, hopes, and dreams with one another, as this will enable you to visualise better times, which will surely come, because nothing lasts forever. There's an old-fashioned word we don't hear so much these days, but I think it expresses what I mean splendidly. Instead of letting adversity divide you – you must *cleave* together

12. Keeping in shape and not letting yourself go

Inevitably our faces and bodies change as we age. We may no longer have pert tits like ripe cherries and our saddlebags and haunches may be somewhat weathered but, again, it's vital to keep in physical shape and not let yourself go for your health's sake, your self-esteem, as well as to please your partner. Shakespeare said, "Love is not love that alters, when it alteration finds" – but get real… how would *you* like it if he morphed into a fat bastard? If you need to get fit, then go for it, and remember you are what you eat – rubbish in equals rubbish out. Quit the fags. Lose some weight. Your body has to last you a lifetime, so respect and look after it well.

Martha, a retired 63-year-old was, by her own admission, a fat and unfit couch potato. Her retired 64-year-old husband, Ian, was a very fit and active man, who particularly enjoyed extreme sports – Martha's idea of absolute horror. Whilst Ian engaged in abseiling and the like, Martha sat at home, knitting, eating chocolate and watching daytime TV. She was also incredibly resentful of Ian going out and about, and these difficulties began to cause arguments between them. Ian felt hemmed in, and Martha felt that Ian was being selfish and that he should know that she was in no condition to join him in these activities. The more she complained, the more Ian felt compelled to escape the retirement prison their formerly happy home had become.

In the end, Martha and Ian decided to go for couples counselling to thrash out their difficulties. It was painful for Martha to hear Ian's point of view but, with the input of their excellent therapist, Martha began to realise that she had to fight her fat and unfitness demons. In doing so, she began to find her own enjoyable physical activities to engage in, such as yoga and dancing. The thought of exercise was worse than the reality of actually doing it, and Martha started to feel better. I pointed out to her that one of Ian's traits, which had actually attracted her in the first place, was his exciting sense of adventure. To curb that now, because she'd let herself go, was injurious to their previously happy relationship.

13. Leave the past behind

You're here NOW, so don't measure yourself against his past. I had a client, a 43-year-old architect called Meri, who in a past relationship, tortured herself by repeatedly and secretly going through her partner's memorabilia and photographs. As if this wasn't bad enough, she then started exercising vigorously on a daily basis, whilst staring at a picture of his past lover, to "motivate" herself. Total and utter madness! He loves you, he's with you now, and his past belongs exactly there, not in the present.

If it bothers either of you to have memorabilia in your home, then you're going to have to work it out between you, and come to some sort of agreement about what to do with it. Much as you might feel like doing so, the inner glow of satisfaction you may feel from throwing out his things will be short-lived when he finds out about it. Trust your partner – so no peeking at his mobile, going through his emails, or listening in on his calls!

An intimate relationship is your greatest teacher – so learn your lessons well and don't quit! It's always way too early in a committed relationship to throw in the towel, unless something totally unacceptable happens, such as violence or an addiction for which your partner refuses to seek help. A great relationship can heal and nurture you in a much healthier way than your birth parent did – it's like a mirror – reflecting the good, the bad, the ugly in both of you. Yes, it's work, but like your post-menopausal vagina – don't allow your relationship to atrophy. If you don't use it, you risk losing it. Being someone's first love is great, being someone's last love is beyond perfect.

WOEs → WOWs (Words of Wisdom)

♥ Don't allow familiarity to breed contempt in your relationship.

♥ A good relationship is about ongoing compromise.

♥ Learn to hear your partner, rather than just listening to him, which is different.

♥ Meditate together and breathe in the good shit – breathe out the bad shit.

♥ Don't allow adversity to cast you asunder – transform it into an opportunity for joint growth.

♥ Never part, nor go to sleep, on a bad note – kiss and make up, even if it's with angry sex.

♥ Laugh with, not at, your partner – it's sexy!

CHAPTER 14

SHORT AND SWEET

And finally...

I hope that, by now, you'll have progressed a long way on your dating journey, and will have found the man of your dreams. To recap, here are the main points of this book, in brief outline.

Finding love is an Inside Job

You can't give of yourself, from an empty place. You have to learn to love yourself before you can love another, and the only way to do this is to learn to take great care of yourself on every level. Nobody else can ever make you feel complete – you must be willing to do The Work on your inner self, before finding outer happiness.

There are no quick fixes, nor satisfactory shortcuts. Self-care doesn't equate to selfishness. If you feel good about yourself, everybody will benefit from this. Include at least one aspect of self-care in your daily routine. As you feel more confident, you'll start to attract healthier partners and will make much wiser, mindful dating choices.

Learn mindfulness meditation

Take the time to learn this fantastic skill. You'll never regret it and every single aspect of your life, emotional and physical health will benefit from it. You don't have to run off to an ashram, nor chant weird mantras. Meditating can be done anywhere, at any time, and will train you to mind the gap between your impulses and responses – wherein lies freedom. Do yourself a favour and embrace this vital tool. It's well worth the initial pain of self-discipline.

Be true to yourself

You're an authentic person – a one-off. There's nobody else on this earth who's like you, so be proud of it! Whilst remaining true to yourself, also be sure to keep an open mind about the type of man you're looking for; your tastes may change, as you continue to work on yourself. Also remain aware of what your historical filters may tell you erroneously about yourself and men. Don't buy into the stereotypes about men or women.

It's never too late to find love

Make sure that you're in the right place in your life to find love – but also remember that finding love has no sell-by date on it. Be humble enough to seek objective input on your dating assets and liabilities from people who have your best interests at heart. Seeking help is a sign of strength and not weakness.

Self-awareness – however you obtain this – allows you to stop repeating the same relationship mistakes, and so offers you a much-improved chance of a different outcome: a healthy, nurturing partner. Make the time to dedicate yourself to searching for your Big Love. Spend your hard-earned cash on yourself and on any practical arrangements you need to make for the care of any dependent children or parents, while you concentrate on your top priority – yourself.

Don't compare your journey to anybody else's

Comparisons are odious and don't serve you. Value your successes and learn from your mistakes, transforming them into learning experiences, rather than a stick to castigate yourself with.

Be compassionate with yourself. Anchor yourself in the present moment by practising mindfulness and don't allow your anxiety to run away with you. Self-pity is ugly – do something for somebody else and you'll soon put your own frustrations into perspective. Be grateful for the good things in your life and focus on these, not the perceived difficulties. Gratitude attracts positivity like a magnet. Stay upbeat. When the going gets tough, remind yourself of where you came from.

Develop a supportive network of female friends

Be selective with whom you keep company. Negativity is infectious, as is positivity. Don't hang out with people who drain you. Seek out women who raise your spirits, not those who diminish or devalue you in any way. You don't need a huge number of acquaintances, but a wise group of discreet women friends – hopefully some of whom are in successful long term relationships – is best. Never dump your close girlfriends when you've found a partner. You owe it to yourself – and your relationship – to keep your network vibrant and evolving.

Bury your baggage before entering a committed relationship

Don't drag all your relationship yesterdays into today, and don't look back and stare. Keep moving forward. Use as many self-help tools as you need to overcome emotional blockages and, if necessary, seek professional help from a good therapist.

Believe you'll find a good man and you most certainly will.

Every stage of your life will demand a different version of you. Now is the time to embrace all your experiences and use them to enhance your present and future. Pain can foster wisdom. Be mindful of your *needs* as they may actually be very different from your *wants* and don't expect the impossible of another person – any more than they should expect this of you.

Make the best of your physical assets

Do as much as is necessary to enhance your physical self, but always remember that this is merely your outer shell – and not who you truly are.

Embrace your age, and don't lie about it. You'll only look like an idiot when you get found out – and think how you'd feel if the shoe were on the other foot. Remember, not everybody lives long enough to have wrinkles on their face and saddlebags on their hips. Change what you can to be happy and healthy, and to improve your confidence – but don't lose track of your personality, nor fall into the trap of trying to look years younger by dressing in an age-inappropriate way, which may result in looking foolish.

Be proactive when seeking love

You have to go out and look for love. It won't come knocking on your door. Men are flattered when a woman shows interest in them. Proactive doesn't mean desperate! Transfer the guts you have in your professional life to your man search. Don't take yourself or what happens too seriously though – give it time. With perseverance, you will succeed. Take it in small steps, set yourself objectives, and review them regularly. This will increase your confidence levels.

If something doesn't stack up – get out

If you smell a dating rat – you're probably correct. Learn to trust your instincts and act on them. Abandon ship. Never put yourself in a dangerous situation at any stage in a relationship. You don't deserve it and you don't have to people please, nor be a chameleon. Inconsistency in a partner is a big warning sign. Don't fudge it in the hope that it will go away – it won't.

Good communication is crucial

Whether you're in the early stages of dating or in a committed relationship, remember that the one issue which can make or break your future is poor communication. Learning the art of good, mindful communication is the lifeblood of your relationship and future happiness. It takes continuing effort; it's worth every ounce of sweat it demands to get this right.

After you've met The One

Remember that everybody has baggage of one sort or another. Maintain realistic expectations of yourself and of him. Nowhere is this truer than in the area of step parenting, which is the hardest job in the world in my opinion. Set boundaries. Keep the romance alive. Always make the effort to continue surprising each other with tender gestures of love. Don't let yourself go physically and if you have, then get back in shape. Learn new things together and with others. Avoid relationship complacency like the plague. Continue to show appreciation for each other and remember that happiness is derived from the small pleasures of life – not necessarily two-carat diamond rings and Aston Martins! Stay calm during adversity and grow through it, rather than allow it to rip you apart. You've waited a long time for each other, now don't you wreck it or allow anybody else to do so. Have fun with one another. Love each other outrageously, and together you'll discover a joie de vivre you'd never have thought possible!

FURTHER RESOURCES

Dating

The International Dating Academy – a one stop shop for people who wish to improve their dating skills

www.internationaldatingacademy.com

Dinner Dates – a social networking company for professional singletons

www.dinnerdates.com

The Vida Consultancy – an exclusive matchmaking company

www.thevidaconsultancy.com/

Rendezvous – a social events company for professional singletons

www.rendezvous-london.com

The Association of British Introduction Agencies – the authoritative voice of the introduction agency

www.abia.org.uk

Spice UK – group activities and holidays for singletons

www.spiceuk.com

Mark Warner – holidays for singletons

www.markwarner.co.uk

Addiction

Alcohol

www.alcoholics-anonymous.org.uk

For families and anybody who is in any way affected by another's alcoholism

www.al-anonuk.org.uk

Sex and love addiction

www.slaauk.org

Co-dependency

www.coda-uk.org

Debt

www.debtorsanonymous.org.uk

Drugs

www.ukna.org

Food

www.oagb.org.uk

Therapy

www.relate.org.uk – offers *counselling* services for every type of *relationship*, nationwide.

www.bacp.co.uk – to find an accredited therapist

www.psychotherapy.org.uk – to find an accredited therapist

Elderly relatives

www.ageconcern.org.uk – support for elderly relatives.

Bereavement

www.crusebereavementcare.org.uk

www.wayfoundation.org.uk – social and support network for men and women widowed up to the age of 50.

Child bereavement

www.tcf.org.uk – largely run by bereaved parents, for bereaved parents, grandparents and siblings.

Lone parents

www.gingerbread.org.uk

Stepfamilies

www.happysteps.co.uk – resources for stepfamilies.

Domestic violence and abuse

www.refuge.org.uk

Mindfulness Meditation

www.bangor.ac.uk/mindfulness – for information on reputable and accredited courses.

General interest courses

www.hotcourses.com – a comprehensive list of thousands of courses, nationwide.

OTHER BOOKS FROM BENNION KEARNY

Finding Your Way Back to YOU: A self-help book for women who want to regain their Mojo and realise their dreams! By Lynne Saint.

Are you at a crossroads in life, lacking in motivation, looking for a new direction or just plain 'stuck'?

Finding your Way back to YOU is a focused and concise resource written specifically for women who have found themselves in any of the positions above.

The good news is that you already have all of the resources you need to solve your own problems; this practical book helps you remove the barriers that prevent this from happening.

Designed as a practical book with an accompanying downloadable journal and weblinked exercises, *Finding Your Way Back to YOU* is an inspiring book that introduces Neuro- Linguistic Programming, and Cognitive Behavioural Therapy techniques for change that are particularly valuable within the coaching context.

> Recognise Who and What is holding you back

> Make a commitment to yourself and your future

> Boost your self-confidence and self-esteem

> Identify and Challenge your limiting beliefs

> Regain your life balance

> Supercharge your self-image

> Get motivated… Achieve your life goals

Now available as an audiobook

The Savvy Traveller Survival Guide by Peter John

Travel is one of our favourite activities. From the hustle of bustle of the mega-cities to sleepy mountain towns to the tranquillity and isolation of tropical islands, we love to get out there and explore the world.

But globe-trotting also comes with its pitfalls. Wherever there are travellers, there are swindlers looking to relieve individuals of their money, possessions and sometimes even more. To avoid such troubles, and to get on with enjoyable and fulfilling trips, people need to get smart. This book shows you how.

The Savvy Traveller Survival Guide offers practical advice on avoiding the scams and hoaxes that can ruin any trip. From no-menu, rigged betting, and scenic taxi tour scams to rental damage, baksheesh, and credit card deceits – this book details scam hotspots, how the scams play out and what you can do to prevent them. *The Savvy Traveller Survival Guide* will help you develop an awareness and vigilance for high-risk people, activities, and environments.

Forewarned is forearmed!

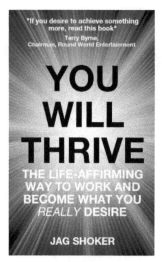

You Will Thrive: The Life-Affirming Way to Work and Become What You Really Desire by Jag Shoker

Have you lost your spark or the passion for what you do? Is your heart no longer in your work or (like so many people) are you simply disillusioned by the frantic race to get ahead in life? Your sense of unease may be getting harder to ignore, and comes from the growing urge to step off the treadmill and pursue a more thrilling *and* meaningful direction in life.

You Will Thrive addresses the subject of modern disillusionment. It is essential reading for people looking to make the most of their talents and be something more in life. Something that matters. Something that makes a difference in the world.

Through six empowering steps, it reveals 'the Way' to boldly follow your heart as it leads you to the perfect opportunities you seek. Through every step, it urges you to put a compelling thought to the test:

You possess the power within you to attract the right people, opportunities, and circumstances that you need to become what you desire.

As you'll discover, if you find the *faith* to act on this power and do the Work required to realise your dream, a testing yet life-affirming path will unfold before you as life *orchestrates* the Way to make it all happen.

Write From The Start: The Beginner's Guide to Writing Professional Non-Fiction by Caroline Foster

Do you want to become a writer? Would you like to earn money from writing? Do you know where to begin?

Help is at hand with *Write From The Start* – a practical must-read resource for newcomers to the world of non-fiction writing. It is a vast genre that encompasses books, newspaper and magazine articles, press releases, business copy, the web, blogging, and much more besides.

Jam-packed with great advice, the book is aimed at novice writers, hobbyist writers, or those considering a full-time writing career, and offers a comprehensive guide to help you plan, prepare, and professionally submit your non-fiction work. It is designed to get you up-and-running fast.

Write From The Start will teach you how to explore topic areas methodically, tailor content for different audiences, and create compelling copy. It will teach you which writing styles work best for specific publications, how to improve your chances of securing both commissioned and uncommissioned work, how to build a portfolio that gets results, and how to take that book idea all the way to publication.

Comprised of 16 chapters, there is information on conducting effective research, book submissions, writing for business, copyright and plagiarism pitfalls, formatting, professional support networks, contracts and agreements, the value of humour, ghostwriting, and much more…

Dr Martin Turner   Dr Jamie Barker

**WHAT BUSINESS CAN
LEARN FROM
SPORT PSYCHOLOGY**
10 Lessons for Peak
Professional Performance

What Business Can Learn From Sport Psychology: Ten Lessons for Peak Professional Performance by Martin Turner and Jamie Barker

"You don't understand anything until you learn it more than one way." Marvin Minsky

How are the best athletes in the world able to function under the immense pressure of competition? By harnessing the potential of their minds to train smart, stay committed, focus, and deliver winning performances with body and mind when the time is right.

The mental side of performance has always been a crucial component for success – but nowadays coaches, teams, and athletes of all levels and abilities are using sport psychology to help fulfil their potential and serve up success.

It goes without saying that business performance has many parallels with sporting performance. But did you realize that the scientific principles of sport psychology, used by elite athletes the world over, are being used by some of the most successful business professionals? Performance – in any context – is about utilizing and deploying every possible resource to fulfil your potential.

In *What Business Can Learn From Sport Psychology* you will develop the most important weapon you need to succeed in business: your mental approach to performance. This book reveals the secrets of the winning mind by exploring the strategies and techniques used by the most successful athletes and professionals on the planet.